THE
ARAB
WINTER

THE ARAB WINTER

A TRAGEDY

NOAH FELDMAN

PRINCETON UNIVERSITY PRESS

PRINCETON AND OXFORD

Published by Princeton University Press
41 William Street, Princeton, New Jersey 08540
6 Oxford Street, Woodstock, Oxfordshire OX20 1TR

press.princeton.edu

Library of Congress Cataloging-in-Publication Data

Names: Feldman, Noah, 1970– author.
Title: The Arab Winter : A Tragedy / Noah Feldman.
Description: Princeton, New Jersey : Princeton University Press, [2020] |
Includes bibliographical references and index.
Identifiers: LCCN 2019030392 (print) | LCCN 2019030393 (ebook) |
ISBN 9780691194929 (hardback) | ISBN 9780691201443 (ebook)
Subjects: LCSH: Arab Spring, 2010– | Arab countries—Politics and
government—21st century.
Classification: LCC DS39.3 .F45 2020 (print) | LCC DS39.3 (ebook) |
DDC 909/.097492708312—dc23
LC record available at https://lccn.loc.gov/2019030392
LC ebook record available at https://lccn.loc.gov/2019030393

British Library Cataloging-in-Publication Data is available

Editorial: Fred Appel and Jenny Tan
Production Editorial: Mark Bellis
Text Design: Lorraine Doneker
Jacket Design: Layla Mac Rory
Production: Erin Suydam
Publicity: James Schneider and Kathryn Stevens

This book has been composed in Arno Pro

Printed on acid-free paper. ∞

Printed in the United States of America

1 3 5 7 9 10 8 6 4 2

For Owen Fiss

CONTENTS

PREFACE

Al-sha'b
Yurid
Isqat al-nizam!

The people
Want
The overthrow of the regime!

These words, chanted rhythmically all over the Arabic-speaking world beginning in January 2011, promised a transformation in the history of the Middle East. For the first time, mass movements of ordinary people sought to take their political fate into their own hands and shape a better future for themselves. The optimism of their aspirations and the bravery of their efforts met with sympathy and excitement around the globe, especially from believers in the value of self-government. The most exciting, revolutionary aspect of the Arab spring was that the people were acting on their own, wresting control away from repressive governments and the international great powers who had long supported them.

Yet as we know today, the electrifying course of events that began in Tunisia, swept through Egypt, touched half a dozen more countries, and eventually reached Syria ultimately brought little good except to the place where it had begun. Slowly, painfully, by fits and starts, the heroic narrative of the Arab spring was transmuted into something much darker.

There is a word for what happens when nobility, hope, and the human capacity to take action run headlong into conflict, error, and the human capacity to inflict horror. We call that tragedy: the reversal that produces in us the distinctive combination of terror and empathy that Aristotle identified as catharsis. In the Arab spring, the poetic call to change was merely the opening chorus of the drama.

It took seven years for the tragedy to play out. And now, from a distance that is short when measured in historical time but long when measured by how much has happened, a consensus view is emerging about the Arab spring. The view can be stated simply: it was doomed to fail. In retrospect, experts and others are saying, there was no truly transformative political self-determination in those countries where people took to the streets and expressed their will to change. Arab popular self-government was a "mirage," a "false dawn."[1] Arabs (or maybe Muslims) were "exceptional" relative to the democratic capacities of other peoples.[2] Seen through this retrospective lens, it is as though the Arab spring never happened—because genuine political action requires achieving power, and the people never actually succeeded in doing that, whatever they may briefly have hoped and believed.

The purpose of this book is to save the Arab spring from the verdict of implicit nonexistence and to propose an alternative account that highlights the exercise of collective, free political action—with all the dangers of error and disaster that come with it. There is no question that, apart from removing a handful of dictators, the Arab spring did not achieve most of its grander aspirations. I do not dispute that in many ways, the Arab spring ultimately made many people's lives worse than they were before. Some of the energies released by the Arab spring were particularly horrifying, including those that fueled the Syrian civil war and the rise of the Islamic State.

Nevertheless, there *was* an Arab spring that led to today's Arab winter. Something—many things—took place. Those things mattered. People whose political lives had been determined and shaped from the outside tried politics for themselves, and for a time succeeded. That this did not lead to constitutional democracy or even to a more decent life for most of those affected is not a reason to believe that the effort was meaningless. To the contrary, the political action undertaken in the course of the Arab spring carried and still carries profound meaning. Failure is always one possible outcome of attempting self-determination. Regardless, the effort mattered for the course of history. And it matters for the future.

In place of the narrative of impotence and impossibility, I want to tell a different story of the arc from spring to winter, from inspired hope to tragic failure. In this account, the Arab spring marked a crucial, historical break from a long era in which empires—Ottoman, European, and American—definitively shaped the course of Arab politics. The participants in the events of the Arab spring and its aftermath took charge of their politics through action. In doing so, they remade and transformed the two big forces that have dominated political ideas in the Arabic-speaking world for the past century, namely Arab nationalism and political Islam.

In what follows, I set out to offer an interpretation of the deep political meaning of the Arab spring and its consequences. This interpretation comprises three main claims, all far-reaching, and all potentially controversial.

My first argument begins with the observation that the Arab spring uprisings marked a new, unprecedented phase in Arab political experience, in which participants engaged in collective action for self-determination that was not conceived primarily in relation to imperial power—neither as the main target of the collective movement nor as its fomenter or supporter. In this important aspect, the Arab spring uprisings differed from the Arab independence movements of the early twentieth century, which were essentially anticolonial. They differed from the Arab revolutions against monarchs, which spanned the years 1920–73 and often had a significant component of anti-imperial ideology. And they differed rather obviously from the constitution making and civil war that followed the imperially initiated U.S. invasion of Iraq.[3]

The core of the claim I wish to make relates to the political significance of this new phase. In my view, the central political meaning of the Arab spring and its aftermath is that it featured Arabic-speaking people acting essentially on their own, as full-fledged, independent makers of their own history and of global history more broadly. Arabs were acting to choose among possible Arab governments; and the governing forces arrayed against them were similarly Arab forces, not empires or imperial proxies. In basic terms, the events took place in a framework defined by Arab choice and Arab power. Inasmuch as such a thing is ever possible in a world of global interaction and interdependence, the Arab spring and the Arab winter were the Arabs' *own*.

That is not to say that imperial powers were not still relevant to the political choices made by Arab actors. The background conditions that shaped the history of Arab political institutions were inflected and shaped by colonialism and imperialism. Protesters in Egypt against Hosni Mubarak wondered whether and how the United States would support the regime. Sunnis in Syria hoped that the United States would intervene militarily to remove Bashar al-Assad from power, as it had already intervened in Libya to defeat Muammar al-Qaddafi. Assad himself ultimately came to rely on a quasi-imperial Russian intervention to defeat the insurgents and ensure his survival.

The point, rather, is that the key decisions—to rise against existing governments, to form new ones, to bring them down—were made from within. They were not motivated or made based on opposition to empire or encouragement from it. Outside forces were relevant to political calculations but did not determine them.

For this reason, the passage from Arab spring to Arab winter should be understood first and foremost as a narrative of self-determination, choice, and consequences, not as a story of heteronomy and external imposition. Moral assessments of credit and demerit, praise and blame, right and wrong must be laid first and foremost at the feet of the participants. According to a discourse shared by many politicians, activists, and academics, the story of modern politics in the Arabic-speaking world has been framed largely in terms of imperial oppression and resistance to it. I am suggesting that the events of the Arab spring and winter warrant a very different framework, one defined by collective political action that was in an important sense autonomous.

The second argument of the book is that Arab nationalism looks very different during today's Arab winter than it did before the Arab spring. On the one hand, the Arab spring demonstrated the existence of a transnational, even pan-Arab sense of cross-border political identification. Previously, the particularities of national experience in different Arabic-speaking states had made it possible and even fashionable to question the existence of such a broad sentiment. The Arab spring recurred in a great number of Arab countries—and it *only* visited Arab states. Political events in some Arab countries had massive spillover effects in others, from the imitative, fast-spreading protests and slogans to post-revolutionary struggles to specific techniques of repression. All these reflected the reality of political identification among and across Arab "people" and "peoples."

On the other hand, within the states where the Arab spring led to major changes, the sense of an existing intraborder Arab nation has been radically undercut, and in some cases destroyed, relative to the pre–Arab spring moment. This collapse of national identity was already prefigured in post-invasion Iraq, with its combination of ethnic (Arab-Kurd) and denominational (Sunni-Shi'i) cleavages. But where the Iraqi experience could be blamed on imperial intervention, the divisions in Libya, Syria, Yemen, and even Egypt cannot be similarly laid at the feet of an occupier seeking to categorize and control a local population. The divisions in the states riven by civil war are ethnic, denominational, interreligious, geographical, tribal, and ideological. Relative homogeneity along one dimension has not stopped other dimensions of division from becoming fault lines in existential struggles for power.

The takeaway from this profound internal division within some Arab states is that Arab nationalism can no longer be said to function as a plausible or compelling ideology for projecting national unity within Arabic-speaking countries. Indeed, nationalism itself looks very much endangered in the entire region as a consequence of this breakdown of state order. Where at one time Lebanon with its history of civil war might have been seen as an outlier relative to other Arab national units, it now looks more like an archetype. Arab countries that have not undergone civil war in the modern era are no longer even a clear majority among all Arab nations.

It matters, I want to suggest, that this breakdown of national identification is a product of collective efforts at self-determination, efforts that led not to unity but to the opposite.

And although imperial powers, especially European ones, undoubtedly played an important part in shaping ethnic, denominational, and tribal divisions in Arabic-speaking countries, those historical influences date back too far to be the immediate causes of contemporary fissiparous tendencies. The realities of contemporary identity have developed during decades of statist ideology, especially the ideologies of Arab nationalism as practiced in Libya, Syria, Iraq, Yemen, and beyond. The key point is that Arab self-determination has crushed the myth of coherent, unified Arab nations with their own individual national identities.

The third major claim I want to advance is that the events that followed the Arab spring fundamentally transformed political Islam—broadly, the set of ideas and movements that aspire to a constitutional order grounded in the shari'a.[4] Prior to the Arab spring, modern, Sunni, political Islam had undergone a nearly twenty-five-year process in which some of its most prominent exponents began to advocate for Arab states to Islamize their political order by democratic, constitutional means. Yet this model, adopted by the Muslim Brotherhood, had not really been tried. Although movements associated with the Brotherhood had participated in government in Jordan and Morocco, in both cases they did so under the effective control of monarchies that severely limit politicians' freedom of action. The closest any Arab state came to instantiating modernized Islamic democratic political government was Iraq, where the constitution enshrines the shari'a alongside democracy and the Shi'i party known as Da'wa has provided all the prime ministers since 2005.

After the fall of the presidential regimes in Tunisia and Egypt, parties associated with the Muslim Brotherhood won pluralities or majorities in both countries. As I shall discuss at length, in Egypt, the Brotherhood ultimately failed or was blocked from effectively governing, and after the military replaced the Brotherhood with Abdel Fattah el-Sisi, the Brotherhood was outlawed and suppressed. The question of causation aside, the Brotherhood's collapse marked a generational end to democratically oriented political Islam not only in Egypt but in the whole of the Arabic-speaking world.

In the shadow of the Brotherhood's collapse, Ennahda, the Brotherhood-affiliated party in Tunisia, gradually remade itself into a liberal Islamic party rather than an exponent of mainstream political Islam. This occurred formally when Ennahda officially abandoned the core, definitional element of Islamism (a term I use interchangeably with political Islam)—the aspiration to make the shari'a into the basis of the state's constitutional order. I will analyze this fascinating and fateful choice later on; here it suffices to say that the successful transition of Ennahda is almost as consequential to the fate of political Islam as the Egyptian Brotherhood's failure. Ennahda's self-transformation itself marks an end to political movements advocating political Islamization through democratic means.

Most strikingly, with the Brotherhood and Ennahda in different ways showing the vulnerabilities of democratically oriented Islamism, the caliphate of the Islamic State entered the global stage in the context of the post–Arab spring civil war in Syria. Unlike the Brotherhood and its affiliates, the Islamic State eschewed democratic values and practices. Its version of political Islam can in fact be interpreted as a conscious rejection of the Brotherhood's modernism and the democratic inclinations to which that modernism eventually led the movement. In contrast, the Islamic State sought to recast political Islam in its recension as entirely continuous with premodern classical Islamic political governance. This was a major move in the trajectory of political Islam. It sustained a functioning state for more than two years, attracting external adherents and achieving some measures of effective governance. But it, too, failed, not because of its murderous brutality but as a result of a sustained military campaign funded by mostly external actors who viewed the Islamic State's utopia as dystopian.

In advancing these three main claims, the book proceeds in a series of five chapters. Chapter 1 explores the transnational commonalities and differences of the basic demands made by the Arab spring protesters. It introduces my argument about self-determination and begins to consider the question of pan-Arab nationalism via the spread of the uprisings and the symbolic and ideological content of their invocations of "the people." This chapter is framed as an inquiry into the meaning of revolutionary political action. In it, I ask: Who were *the people*? What did they *want*? Who was supposed to perform the *overthrow*? What *regime* was meant to go, and what was meant to replace it?

Regime change was not the protesters' only mantra, needless to say. Alongside demands that took the imperative form "Leave!" (*irhal!*), protesters called for "Freedom, dignity, social justice," in the words of one particularly popular rhyming slogan. Many other slogans have received attention in the secondary academic literature.[5] The reason to focus on the core insistence that "the people want the overthrow of the regime" is that most of the other demands for change, though sincerely meant, were vague and general, not specific and concrete. Indeed, even the leading slogan was riven with uncertainty. The protesters did not say who would remove the existing regime. Nor did they specify what form of government would bring about their demands. Democracy went unmentioned, surely by design and certainly with important consequences.

Taking Egypt as its focal point, chapter 2 seeks to evaluate moral meaning. Developing my argument about self-determination, I ask here about the agency of "the people." Did the people act or speak when they created the conditions for the

Egyptian army to remove Hosni Mubarak? I argue that the Egyptian people did speak and did engage in genuine political action. Yet I go on to maintain that if we accept that the people called for Mubarak to go, then we must also accept (despite the existence of deep state and military support for the removal protests) that the people spoke when they invited the army to remove Mohamed Morsi, the democratically elected post-revolutionary president. This was a colossal moral and practical error, I suggest—yet one for which the Egyptian people bear responsibility.

In chapter 3, I take on Syria and consider the question of responsibility for the disastrous civil war that followed the Arab spring there. Here the focus is first on my larger claim that the Arab spring should not be understood in terms of imperialism and second on my claim about the dynamics of the breakdown of the national state. My suggestion in this chapter is that responsibility for the Syrian civil war lies not with the United States or past imperial powers like France but with the domestic Syrian structures of authority and identity that framed the conflict. In particular, fault lies with the Syrian configuration of a dictatorship dominated by a single denominational minority, the ʿAlawis. Given that power structure, which emerged over a fifty-year period, Sunni, ʿAlawi, and Christian Syrians alike bore a heavy burden of presenting one another with options for avoiding state collapse and civil war. Those options, however, did not emerge, or at least did not emerge with sufficient clarity and plausibility to avoid a violent Sunni-ʿAlawi conflict—itself evidence of the failure and passing of the Syrian version of Baʿthist Arab nationalism.

Chapter 4 addresses the Islamic State, offering a reading of that phenomenon that emphasizes the ideology of the caliphate as a rejectionist version of political Islam. My claim is that the

Islamic State is best understood as a utopian, revolutionary-reformist movement that attained success locally and globally because of its appeal to jihadi-Salafi Muslims who were disappointed or disillusioned with other, modernist versions of political Islam. Although dystopian when viewed from the outside, the Islamic State reflected its members' intentional, articulated aspiration to self-determining political action. The Islamic State did not just happen and was not foisted on all its members by compulsion. Many joined by choice. In this way, the Islamic State belongs squarely to the Arab spring moment. It was an attempt by some Arabs and Muslims to make their political fate for themselves—albeit in horrific form. Its ideals—and perversions—express a rejection of the failed movement for Islamic democracy, the same movement that also failed when the Muslim Brotherhood government was toppled in Egypt.

Last, in chapter 5, I describe the mixed yet nonetheless remarkable success of Tunisia—a success that makes the other parts of the Arab spring all the more tragic because it shows their failure was not always inevitable. Tunisia, I will suggest, succeeded largely because its people and their leadership took political responsibility for the consequences of their actions rather than seeking help from outside or hoping for internal forces to save them from themselves. Their orientation reflected, heroically, the sense of autonomous collective action that I identify in my first strand of argument as constitutive of the Arab spring. What is more, Tunisians displayed an internal national cohesion even in the face of deep political division, and hence are the exception that proves the rule of Arab national collapse. The consequence was the compromise-driven creation of a liberal Islamic democratic movement, one that deeply influenced the Tunisian constitution. This phenomenon forms an important step in my broader argument about the transformation of political Islam.

Yet I conclude that even Tunisia's noteworthy accomplishments have so far failed to address the economic and social problems that fed the Arab spring where it began. Tunisia solved a problem—but not the problem that caused its revolution.

Having introduced the book, I owe the reader—particularly the specialist reader—a word about what it is and is not. Throughout, my intention is to illuminate themes of political meaning associated with concrete human actions in the political sphere. I am not primarily concerned to explain every detail of *what* happened—the first question of history—or structurally *why* it happened—the dominant question of political science. This book therefore is not an attempt to explain precisely why the Arab spring took place when it did or why the outcomes differed from place to place. These questions have received ample attention from other writers and will receive more in the future.[6] My views on them are sometimes implicit in the text, but this is not a work of history or of structural political science and should not be taken for one.

My constant question is, rather, *what does it mean* that these things happened? This is the sort of question that the philosopher Hannah Arendt so influentially asked about the American and French revolutions,[7] and indeed about political action itself. To answer the question of meaning, one must necessarily consider the history and structure of events. As a result, I have relied here often on the work of historians, journalists, and political scientists. But the focus of my approach is always on the interpretation of events in the effort to make them meaningful. My theses draw much more on normative arguments about freedom, responsibility, autonomy, possibility, success, and failure than on chronology or causation or contributing factors. I want to encourage you, the reader, to consider a whole complex of ideas that might change your overall sense of what the Arab spring meant and what the Arab winter portends.

The exploration I undertake in this book is indebted not only to Arendt's question but also to her distinctive conception of political action. As she famously argued, action "corresponds to the human condition of plurality, to the fact that men, not Man, live on the earth and inhabit the world."[8] What she called "plurality," and we might call *collective* action, is, she said, "specifically *the* condition . . . of all political life."[9] Through political action, individuals acting together create the lasting stories that give their lives permanence and meaning. As will become evident, I read the Arab spring very much through this lens of collective meaning-making, particularly when I seek to make sense of who the people were and in what ways they may have acted together.

For Arendt, people who engage in genuine collective political action are exercising freedom in the truest sense. Freedom for Arendt is not reducible to traditional free choice or free will. It is, rather, a manifestation of "the new beginning inherent in birth," when "the newcomer possesses the capacity of beginning something anew, that is, of acting."[10] This notion of freedom should be visible in my exploration of how the Arab spring and its aftermath developed in relation to outside, non-Arab imperial powers. As Arendt put it, freedom "has always been spatially limited." Seen in terms of the realm of political action, the "spaces of freedom" appear as "islands in a sea or as oases in a desert."[11]

Finally, for Arendt the value of political action is "intrinsic; it lies neither in the achievement of goals nor in the maintenance of life." Rather than being measured in terms of success or failure, the true worth of political action "can be judged only by the criterion of greatness."[12] Political action is to be measured by greatness "because it is in its nature to break through the commonly accepted and reach into the extraordinary." And greatness in turn "can only lie in the performance itself and neither in its motivation nor its achievement."[13] In what follows, I seek to assess the political action of the Arab spring and its aftermath in the light of this criterion, which I sometimes also call "nobility," rather than in the more conventional political science language of regime success or regime failure.

In the interests of disclosure, it may also be worth adding that my own stake in the account and argument offered here grows from almost two decades of trying to interpret the trajectory of political developments in the Islamic world in general and the Arabic-speaking world in particular—and from my efforts as an engaged outsider seeking to enable both liberal and Islamic constitutionalism in the Middle East and North Africa. Writing in 2003, before the U.S. invasion of Iraq, I predicted that free elections in Arabic-speaking countries would lead to experiments in Islamic democracy, and I encouraged the United States to let those experiments run their course in the name of democratic self-determination.[14] In 2004, after a truncated stint as constitutional advisor to the Coalition Provisional Authority in Iraq, I explored the ethical consequences of the Iraq invasion and what already appeared as the contradictions and dire failures of the occupation that followed.[15] In 2008, I tried to deepen the continuing debate over Islamic democracy by offering some hypotheses about how classical Islamic constitutional design had worked, how it had failed, and what challenges it would have to overcome in order to solve contemporary governance challenges.[16]

Since 2011, I have watched Islamic democracy rise and fall with stunning speed in Egypt and observed the antidemocratic ideology of the Islamic State drive its own horrific cycle of death and destruction. In Tunisia, I experienced firsthand the alternative of gradual, compromise-driven constitutional politics, complete with the liberalization of the leading Islamist party there.* One epoch in Arab political history has given way to another, or so I am arguing. What has emerged does not give cause for optimism in the short or even medium term. As an observer and occasional participant, I feel no longer young and idealistic but chastened and middle-aged. Nevertheless, midlife demands meaning-making as much as or more than does youth.

Tragedy, as I depict it here, is not simply destiny—at least not always. To be sure, there is an ancient strand of tragic storytelling that depicts the arc of tragedy as inevitable, with the protagonists' ends already predetermined by their stars. But there is also another strand that defines tragedy precisely by the notion that the protagonists make choices based on their individual characters and by their actions participate in the construction of their fates.[17] As Aristotle put it, "with character, precisely as in the structure of events, one should always seek necessity or probability."[18] The "or" in his statement allows for the possibility that the outcome of tragedy need not be necessary. Probability leaves room for different results.

In this book, I mostly emphasize probability rather than necessity. I portray the protagonists of the Arab spring and winter as political actors participating fully and even autonomously in the shaping of the events described. The creation of political

---

* I made half a dozen visits to Tunis during the key period of constitutional negotiations with my associate, Duncan Pickard. We spent extensive time in conversation with members of the constituent assembly, learning from them, discussing ideas, and offering hundreds of suggestions. It was a privilege to be welcomed as a guest into the drafting and dining rooms of the Bardo, where formal and informal negotiations took place.

meaning, I suggest, is one path that can follow from making choices that determine the course of one's own life. Freedom in the deepest sense comes from taking action, and taking responsibility for the consequences.

Yet at the same time I do not deny the powerful, and at times nearly overwhelming, effects of background structures of power and politics on humans striving to become agents of their political lives. In particular, chapter 3 on the emergence of the Syrian civil war acknowledges, as it must, the enormous difficulties for successful political resolution that were created by the denominational structures of Syrian politics. Sometimes tragedy really does resemble necessity. But it is no less ennobling for all that.

This book thus tells a new story of the Arab spring and proposes a new set of meanings both for its events and for the winter that has followed. That meaning is more moral than it is historical. To recognize the presence of genuine political action in the Arab spring is to reject a narrative of nihilism in favor of a call to political responsibility. It is time to recognize that the future of the Arabic-speaking world is and ought to be made by the people who live there, not from the outside. Their successes and failures will be, and must be, their own.

CHAPTER 1

THE PEOPLE WANT

Who were the "people" who wanted the overthrow of their regime?

The word *sha'b* is particularly resonant in modern Arabic. Indeed, it is one of the most powerful and layered words in the contemporary political vocabulary. Its Qur'anic antecedents stem from a famous verse (49:13): "O mankind, indeed We have created you from male and female and made you peoples and tribes that you may know one another." The "peoples" (*shu'ub*) of the verse are plural. In contrast, the "people" of the modern Arabic *sha'b* is singular—and takes a singular verb.

The modern resonance of the Arabic word for "people" lies in Arab nationalism, an intellectual and social movement with origins in the late nineteenth and early twentieth centuries. This movement posited the existence of an identifiable Arab nation, made up (in its grandest reach) of all Arabic speakers from Morocco in the west to Iraq in the east. Sometimes this body was characterized as the "Arab people" (*al-sha'b al-'arabi*), sometimes as the "Arab peoples" (*al-shu'ub al-'arabiya*).[1] For that people or community of peoples, hitherto unknown to history under a single unified term, Arab nationalism prescribed a nation—and ideally, a single, overarching nation-state.

The dream of a single Arab nation-state never came to pass. From the end of World War I and the Versailles peace treaty forward, the trope of the Arab people or peoples has always been reflected through the existence of multiple states that shared and contested the self-description and sometimes the political appellation "Arab." Thus the citizens of the individual states of the Arabic-speaking world might describe themselves as the people of Egypt or Syria or Tunisia, while simultaneously continuing to think of themselves as part of a greater Arab nation.

It is significant that the "people" of the chants that began in January 2011 were not subdesignated by the states to which they belonged (as in, "the Tunisian people want") or explicitly named as "Arab" (as in, "the Arab people want"). From a literary standpoint, the explanation may be that the chant was borrowed from a poem by the Tunisian author Abu al-Qasim al-Shabbi, which begins (rendered literally), "If some day the people wanted life."[2] It is also true that the phrase scanned well in Arabic without the added syllables of a national or pan-national designation.

But it is also worth noting that, within a short time of the initial Tunisian protests against the Ben Ali regime, the term "Arab" in the phrase "Arab spring" was identifiably if not deliberately dual. On the one hand, Tunisians and then Egyptians, Syrians, Libyans, and so forth were demanding change in their own particular countries. When they called themselves "the people," they were speaking as citizens of the states they constituted. On the other hand, by self-consciously echoing the claims of other Arabic-speaking protesters in other countries, the chanters were suggesting that a broader people—implicitly, the Arab people or peoples—were seeking change from the regime or regimes (more on this shortly) that were governing them.

The fact that the people were seeking change first of all in their own countries reflected the institutional realities of Middle

Eastern states in the early 2010s. Although different actors in different Arabic-speaking states were often politically entwined, none was fully interdependent: to call for change in one country was not necessarily to call for change elsewhere, or everywhere. In the first instance, chanting Tunisians wanted Ben Ali out, Egyptians wanted Mubarak to go, and Syrians wanted to rid themselves of Bashar.

It is a crucially important fact of the Arab spring and its aftermath that the distinctive institutional arrangements, politics, and demographics of individual countries operated more or less on their own—and produced drastically divergent outcomes. Egypt and Syria and Tunisia look radically different from one another today because they were different countries, whose differences outweighed their similarities when it came to the realities of change. The same is also true of Libya, Yemen, Bahrain, and the other countries where the Arab spring had important effects.[3]

Yet the broader, pan-Arab national aspect of the call to change also must not be minimized or gainsaid. For one thing, very early in 2011, the movement that seemed to be spreading from country to country came to be called the *Arab* spring. It manifested itself to one degree or another in essentially every Arabic-speaking country, including those where it had little to no chance of making a substantial impact, such as Saudi Arabia. And it did not spread to non-Arabic-speaking countries in the region, such as Turkey and Iran, which have experienced separate and distinct protest movements of their own on their own very different timing.*

---

* Israel is, as usual, a complicated partial exception. The timing of the "social justice" protests that began there in July 2011 clearly had *something* to do with the Arab spring. The protesters' identification of social justice echoed Arab spring protesters' chant for "freedom, dignity, and social justice." Yet the Israeli protests notably did not call for the "overthrow of the regime." They followed hard on the huge

That is no coincidence. The phenomenon of the Arab spring turned out to be distinctively and uniquely Arab in scope. By extension, the protesters' repeated invocation of the "people" in different places implied a transnational Arab identity, or if you prefer, a broader Arab nationalism that connected the Arab "peoples" to one another. Each of the groups of people in different countries chanted the same Arabic slogan referring to the "people"—using the same resonant words, in the same language, transcending different dialects.[4] Other slogans were also shared, to be sure, sometimes in the same words, sometimes with variations. But the slogan asserting peoplehood distinctively stands for the iterative, shared, cross-border process of diffusion, imitation, and common identification.

The contagion of the protests from one Arabic-speaking country to another was also at the same time the product of Arabic media, especially satellite news stations like Al Jazeera. Those stations not only broadcast across borders but, by doing so, have maintained and transformed the ideas and rhetoric of Arab peoplehood. In the discursive space of pan-Arab media, the Arab "peoples" are encouraged, consciously and unconsciously, to participate in common experiences and aspirations. The Al Jazeera phenomenon of common identification across borders, shaped by language and culture, previously had been the subject of much academic discussion.[5] But it had never before been demonstrated through actual political action, repeated across borders in the performance of a script that was learned in the

---

anti-austerity protests that took place across Spain beginning on May 15, 2011, and continuing into the summer. And when the Occupy movement began to draw attention in September 2011 in New York, the Israeli protest movement began to resemble that movement far more than the Arab spring protests. Compare Daniel Monterescu and Noa Shaindlinger, "Situational Radicalism: The Israeli 'Arab Spring' and the (Un)Making of the Rebel City," *Constellations*, February 26, 2013.

first instance through satellite television, if supplemented by the Internet and emergent social media.[6]

Having identified the complexity of the correct level to identify "people" protesting, however, does not resolve the question of who the people were. Rather, it opens a deeper, more fundamental aspect of the same question. When some people form a group and take to the streets and claim to be *the* people, are they? What if the group has no single, stable membership? How many protesters does it take for us to begin to think that "the people" is speaking? Are numbers part of the answer at all?

In approaching this delicate and important question, it is useful to distinguish two different methods of approaching it, which will in turn yield two different kinds of answers. One is historical, sociological, and descriptive. The other is political, philosophical, and normative.

The historical approach begins with the background assumption that "the people" is an abstraction, not a concrete object. The historian Edmund Morgan's classic account of the rise of the idea of popular sovereignty in England and America is called *Inventing the People*.[7] The title more or less sums it up: the "people" do not exist as a natural fact. They and their capacity to act collectively must be invented.

Seen from this perspective, it can never be historically accurate to say that "the people" were gathered in a public square to demand change. To the contrary, as a historical-descriptive matter, there are only individuals and groups *claiming* to speak in the name of the people or on their behalf. Even if every single citizen of the country turned out to chant, the citizens' claim to be the people would still be an abstraction rather than historical reality. The artifact to be studied is the claim to representative peoplehood—and the human beings, existing in that time and space, who make it.[8]

A related descriptive way to look at the question, one that draws on literary and cultural theory, is to say that individuals and groups like those who gathered in the Arab spring are engaged in a *performance* of peoplehood.[9] This approach depicts the actors as undertaking certain actions and saying certain words that are both familiar and ever-changing. Background cultural beliefs and collective memories function like scripts that enable the acts and words to create what the participants understand as speaking for the "people."*

In addressing recent events, this descriptive approach would turn to sociologists in order to figure out who were the specific people chanting that "the people" wanted the overthrow of the regime—and to cultural and literary historians to understand what they were thinking when they did so. The sociologists would be prepared to draw on all the tools available to make sense of contemporaneous events: not only news reports but data drawn from social media, film, surveys, mobile phone providers, and interviews. If police and intelligence archives eventually open, those might also provide rich sources of exploration for future historians. The goal of the inquiry would be to find particular individuals and then generalize about them—to find out not only who, exactly, joined protests but also what *kinds* of people they were, categorized by class, sex and gender, religious and ethnic denomination and viewpoints, and of course political beliefs and attitudes.

It must be said that answering these sociological questions for, say, Egypt, Syria, and Tunisia is extremely challenging—despite

---

* It is possible for this literary-cultural approach to be deployed in a normative vein, not only descriptively. But for my purposes I will classify it here with the descriptive side of the divide because most theorists of performativity are skeptical of normative-philosophical claims about things like peoplehood.

the fact that these events occurred in the past decade and that
many of the participants are still alive and able to speak. Historians of the French Revolution, who have grappled with similar
questions when seeking to understand different actors who
claimed to speak in the name of the people, face what is in certain ways a far more technically challenging problem, since the
people in question are long dead and records are incomplete.[10]
Knowing who, exactly, stormed the Bastille is notoriously difficult. Yet the very multitude of sources available to us in considering contemporaneous events makes the challenge of determining who protested during the Arab spring almost as hard.
The sheer quantity of data makes it difficult to justify generaliza-
tions. And if the sociologists do try to generalize, we can be sure
that some people who were participants in the events will talk
back and tell them they are wrong—a problem that historians
of the eighteenth century do not face.

Nevertheless, we can try our best to apply the historical-
sociological approach to the Arab spring and what followed. In
doing so, we have to consider the changing composition of
crowds and the competing claims of protesters in different waves,
especially in Egypt. We have to let certain representative views
or voices stand in as shorthand for others, running the risk of
error and misrepresentation in doing so. Yet some such analysis
seems to me necessary to discussing the events of the Arab spring
and their aftermath. It would be frustrating and to a degree ir-
relevant if we were to consider the dramatic arc of the story solely
from the point of view of abstractions.

Applying literary and cultural-historical approaches to the
Arab spring is also challenging in its own way. The slogans
chanted by the protesters can offer us tantalizing textual mark-
ers of their ideas. The size and timing of the protests—political-
cultural happenings aimed to change the world—also cry out

to be interpreted, almost as if these, too, were texts. It is impossible to engage the Arab spring seriously without trying to place these words and acts in the context of history, politics, and meaning-making in the Arabic-speaking world over the past century or more. At the same time, the work of interpretation is inevitably incomplete and necessarily affected by our own commitments, beliefs, and values.

For these reasons, and others, it is therefore also worth considering a different, alternative method of addressing the question, one rooted in normative theories of politics and philosophy. This approach begins with a different presupposition than the historical-descriptive. It assumes that, under some circumstances, it does make sense to talk about the people and what they want. The people, after all, are the demos in democracy. "The rule of the people" is only a coherent description of a form of government if it is possible to speak about "the people" governing themselves. Similarly, if we want to criticize autocracy or other unattractive forms of government, we must be able to describe who rules in them in some relation to the rule of the people.

Political theorists, the philosophers who make it their business to talk about government, are perfectly aware of historians' distrust of their categories. But they are not deterred—because what they are after is something different from simple description. Political theory asks: What is the right way to govern? This normative question, focused on what ought to be done and answered in terms of good and bad, cannot be answered purely by positive, factual analysis. It requires norms and values. And to get at norms and values, we need precisely the abstractions that historians like to break down.

Thus, a political theorist asking who were the people seeking political change wants to know primarily whether those individuals had a *convincing* or *legitimate* claim to speak on behalf of the rest of the population of citizens. Raw numbers or other empirical facts may contribute to a normative analysis of what counts as genuine representativeness. But the numbers and demographics alone will never be enough. They must be processed through a normative framework.

That framework is what allows us to ask not only what happened in the Arab spring and its aftermath but also what we should think about. It allows us to evaluate political developments in the light of justice and well-being. Without it, we could not make a judgment distinguishing the good of constitutional democracy in Tunisia from the circularity of Egypt or the evils of brutal civil war in Syria. Historians, of course, make such evaluative judgments all the time—mostly without admitting it. But the real basis for their judgments is often their own implicit political theory.

In what follows, I am going to make lots of judgments—and try to argue for them. A grand history of the trajectory from Arab spring to Arab winter will be desirable in the future. But the events are too close in time for such a history. Besides, I would not be the right person to write it. I am too bound up in my own contemporaneous attempts to understand what has been happening to judge events. I am also too concerned about the post-winter future to adopt the disinterested attitude that would be required to seek after historical objectivity, that unattainable goal historians pursue despite knowing it can never be reached.

Given these circumstances, I am going to combine history and philosophy, empirical analysis and normative judgment. I will try when possible to say which I am doing. But that is also not a perfectly attainable goal because the categories can run together. I care about who were "the people" claiming to be the people. I also care about how peoplehood matters for judging their claims, achievements, and failures.

Want—and Will

"The people want." In Arabic, as noted, the collective noun takes the singular verb. If it did not sound awkward in English I would translate it as "the people wants." It is noteworthy that in American English, some collective nouns do take singular verbs. Americans would not pause for a moment at the formulation "the team wants"—even though British English mandates the plural verb for the collective noun pretty much universally. Why "people" retains its verbal plurality in American English is an intriguing topic that might not be completely digressive—especially if the reason has to do with "We the People" of the U.S. Constitution who, according to the verbs in the preamble, take plural verbs ("do ordain and establish"). For our purposes, it should be enough to emphasize that, grammatically speaking, the *sha'b* expresses itself with a singular voice.

The Arabic verb *yurid* comes with its own linguistic heritage. In addition to "want," it also means wish, desire, or plan. The noun form of the verb is *irada*, which in medieval Arabic signifies will, especially the divine Will or that of a ruler. Translated into formal political theory terms, the chant might reasonably be interpreted as "the people *will* the overthrow of the regime." Indeed, some English translations of the Shabbi poem mentioned earlier render the same verb as "will."

"Will" as opposed to "want" matters—because it immediately suggests that the chant refers to "the will of the people" (*iradat al-sha'b*).[11] And in the political theory of the modern era, at least from Rousseau and the *volonté générale* onward, the will of the people stands for the core intellectual content of democracy: the idea that the will of the people should determine the form of government and the identity of the governors.[12]

Popular will is thus deeply intertwined with the related idea of popular sovereignty. By invoking the one, the Arab spring protesters were compactly suggesting that they were undertaking to introduce the other. In the face of sovereignty exercised by autocratic governments that (in many cases) purported to speak in the name of the people, the "people" were purporting to speak for themselves.

Taken in this sense, "the people want the overthrow of the regime" comes to sound like a declaration of the popular will to take government out of the hands of the governors and transfer it into the hands of the people and the representatives they would subsequently choose. In terms of political theory, this rationale sounds very much like the theory of the right to self-determination. A group of people—leave aside the question of exactly who they are—claims the right to engage in the formative act of self-government. In the instances of Tunisia, Egypt, and Syria, there was no implied claim to be constituting a new *nation* deserving of recognition. Rather, the claim was that the "people" were exercising their right to self-determination by taking power from the existing government and reassigning it.

The historian-sociologist would immediately want to ask who was making this grand claim on behalf of the "people." But from the standpoint of political theory, the most pressing question is whether the claim was legitimate and correct. And here it seems important to note that most democratic political theory strongly supports the idea that the people may legitimately seize power from unjust and undemocratic rulers. Indeed, such an exercise of what may be termed the right to revolution is very close to the central pillar of democratic theory itself.

The basic idea, derived most importantly from the work of John Locke in his *Second Treatise of Government*,[13] is that legitimate government originates in the consent of the governed and is limited by the individual's incapacity to delegate unalienable rights to anyone else. Under this framework, government that is not derived from consent (whether actual or hypothetical), and that fails to recognize basic rights, loses its legitimacy and may justifiably be replaced. Looking at the autocratic presidential republics of the Arab world (I do not speak of the monarchies), it was difficult to escape the conclusion that Lockean conditions of consent and respect for basic rights had been grossly violated. Thus, a right to revolution must have existed in those countries, if it ever exists anywhere.

This brings us back around to the normative question of whether the protesters in these countries should be understood to have acted on behalf of "the people." Seen from a broadly Lockean democratic perspective, it arguably does not matter that the protesters were not elected and may not have been representative of the broader public from the standpoint of demographics or political preferences. The protesters were nonetheless right—right to say that the government was illegitimate, and therefore right to call for something else *in the name of the people.*

To determine if you share this normative, philosophical intuition, ask yourself: What did you think or feel when you first learned of the crowds gathering in Tunisia, Egypt, and beyond? Did you feel uplifted, sympathetic, moved? Did you believe that the governments against which they were rising were illegitimate and oppressive?

If your answer is yes, then (I want to argue) you share a basic commitment to the value and meaning of popular democratic political action. To have had that feeling of sympathy, one had to have believed that the existing governments were bad and illegitimate and that the people had the right to replace them.

Although it is not necessary for my argument, I would also specu-
late that on close introspection, nearly everyone reading these
words shares some version of this belief—readers in Arabic-
speaking countries and Western liberal democracies and even
(or especially) in nondemocratic countries elsewhere.

To be sure, you are entitled to have had second thoughts.
You might have worried from the start about what would happen if the existing governments fell and what that would
mean for peace and security within the Arab countries or in the
region. But that consequentialist concern is separate and distinct from the initial intuition, which is derived from a core
commitment to the democratic ideal of just, consent-based
self-government.

Notice that to share this intuition, you need not have gone
through the process of trying to determine exactly who was
claiming to speak on behalf of the people. Identity and representativeness mattered less—much less—than that the governments actually deserved to go. Indeed, one might even think that
what qualifies a group to speak on behalf of the people is that the
group is making a normatively correct argument about the
people's right to self-govern under conditions of freedom.

This is still a separate question from whether a group claiming to be the people should have the capacity to choose what
government would replace an unjust one, or whether such a
group would have the right to replace a genuinely democratic
government that was in fact chosen by the people. My rather
minimal argument here is only that, where we can all agree that
a government is not based on consent and does not respect
rights, any group that presents itself as speaking on behalf of the
people may legitimately claim to do so when the content of its
speech is to point out the illegitimacy of the government and call
for its replacement.

Overthrow

Is that, in fact, what the protesters were calling for? We turn now to the content of the "will" expressed by "the people." Here, we encounter a paradox.

In the chant we have been assessing, the protesters called for the "overthrow" or the "fall" of the regime. But they did not specify who would overthrow it or bring it down. The basic formulation was ambiguous with respect to agency: the people wanted something to occur but did not say that *they* intended to make it happen.

The paradox is that a people acting on the basis of its own will must logically reserve to *itself* the authority to change the regime. That is, the people are the only legitimate source of revolutionary action. Yet the people held back, at least in the chant, from taking an active role in doing so. They expressed their will, but not necessarily their will to act. The ambiguous formulation hinted that the people might be willing themselves *to be acted upon* passively by someone else who would overthrow the regime.

Lest you think that I am placing too much interpretive emphasis on this possible passive reading, let me support this claim by suggesting that the passive formulation had some tactical value. The Arab spring uprising for the most part consisted of peaceful protests rather than attempts to take over the reins of political power by force.* The protests' goal from the start was to produce public pressure on autocratic rulers that would

---

* I do not mean to overstate the case. On January 28, 2011, the so-called "Friday of anger," Egyptian protesters burned and looted the headquarters of Mubarak's National Democratic Party as well as police stations around the country. The interior ministry and national television station, more traditional objects of coup d'état takeovers, were also attacked. But in the main, the Arab spring protests were framed in

result in voluntary withdrawal from office. Tunisia was, in this and other things, the model. Faced with the magnitude and continuation of the protests, Ben Ali withdrew, apparently voluntarily.

I do not mean to criticize the protesters for seeking voluntary, peaceful transitions rather than actively trying to seize power in the name of the people. To the contrary, the peaceful nature of the Arab spring protests (peaceful, that is, on the side of the protesters) deserves to be admired and complimented. The protesters surely understood that direct confrontation in the form of attacks on government facilities would backfire, invoking and perhaps justifying violent repression from the governments being challenged. In this sense, calling for the overthrow of the regime without directly attempting to bring it down can be seen as moderation, wisdom, and restraint.

Yet the same restraint also hinted at an invitation to other actors—not the people—to step into the breach. If the people were *calling* for the overthrow of the regime, but not proposing to do it themselves, then by implication they were calling *for someone else* to bring down the regime. That someone else could have been any politically elite actor with the capacity to make change. But in Egypt, as in Syria and elsewhere, there was only one institutional actor powerful enough to be a credible candidate to overthrow the regime: the army.

I want to emphasize the fateful nature of this implicit invitation to the army. The entire course of the Arab spring in Egypt was shaped (I might almost say, determined) by this idea and the reality it reflected and helped generate. The protesters could be understood as expressing their collective will not that they

---

the mode of "color revolutions," not coups in the manner previously more common in the history of the Arabic-speaking countries.

overthrow the regime but that the military respond to their call by doing so.

Notice that the "people" asking the military to bring down the regime reflects more than a practical recognition that only the military would have the forceful capacity to do so. It also normatively recognizes the military as an actor obligated morally or politically to act on behalf of the people. The implicit political theory of the chant, as I am reading it, is that there is a direct relationship of delegation from the people to the army. The people wills; the army acts. This implicit theory was made more explicit by another hopeful slogan that was also heard in the early days of the protests in Cairo: "The army and the people are one hand."[14]

Taking this observation a step further, it is possible to uncover an unstated assumption about political authority in the words of the protesters, at least in Egypt and perhaps elsewhere. Under this vaguely recognizable theory, the military functions as the executive arm of the will of the people. In this sense, the army is supposed to act as the guarantor of legitimate government.

This is not the place to explore fully whether such a theory of civilian-military relations could be defended in principle. If this indeed was the implicit theory of many of the protesters in Egypt, it would not have been entirely unique. From Turkey to Latin America it is possible to find variants on such a picture.

For my purposes, it should be enough to note the extreme implausibility of such a theory as a portrayal of civilian-military relations *in Egypt*. For well over half a century, Egypt had been ruled by a series of dictators, each of whom came out of the military. In other words, in Egypt, the military could not plausibly be described as an institutional delegate of the people capable of acting according to its will in displacing unjust government—because the military was itself the power source and origin of the government in question.

To be sure, the same paradoxical call for "the overthrow of the regime" was made in Syria, with different results. Perhaps the protesters, most of them Sunni Arabs, initially hoped the military would remove Bashar al-Assad from power, even though most senior officers were 'Alawi like Bashar himself. But it soon became clear that Bashar would not be brought down from within. In the complicated period that followed—which I will explore further in chapter 3—a growing number of Syrian Sunnis began to take up arms against the regime.

The Syrian rebellion, which eventually turned into part of the Syrian civil war, was therefore not passive in the sense I have been describing. That is, its participants were not in the first instance calling on institutional actors *within* the state to bring down the regime. Although they undoubtedly sought outside help from Western powers in their fight, and indeed may have been gambling on such assistance (in the shadow of the Libyan experience)* when they took up arms, the Syrian rebels were trying to become the active agents of overthrow, not the enablers of an overthrow process that they would endorse.

Yet it also must be noticed that from the moment they took up arms, the Syrian rebels were engaged in a different social and political practice from that undertaken by the peaceful protesters who initiated the Arab spring in Tunisia, Egypt, and elsewhere. They were undertaking the distinct and vastly more dangerous step of violent rebellion against a regime they deemed illegitimate. Although voices in the Syrian National Council initially called for peaceful resistance, from the time the war began

---

* Libyans resorted to force earlier than Syrians, but they did so, it seems fair to say, only after Qaddafi's forces used force against them.

in earnest, those involved were implicitly choosing not to identify with the tradition of mass nonviolent antigovernment protest that goes back to Gandhi's anti-imperial movement and can
be traced through the so-called color revolutions of the early
2000s. In a way, the Syrian rebels were no longer in the realm of
"the people want the overthrow of the regime." They had gradually, but knowingly, entered the realm of war.

The Regime

What "regime" did the protesters want overthrown? In Arabic
as in English, the word "regime" has two simultaneous meanings
in politics: one specific, the other general. "Regime" can refer to
the particular configuration of people exercising power in a given
place: thus, the Ben Ali regime, the Mubarak regime, the Assad
regime. The word "regime" can also refer, more technically, to a
type of government: the regime of autocracy, the regime of democracy, the regime of monarchy. The second meaning describes
a form of rule—in principle, a form of rule that can be observed
in different places and times.

Hence, when protesters called for "the overthrow of the regime," they were certainly calling for the removal of the particular governments in their specific countries. They wanted Ben
Ali and Mubarak and Bashar al-Assad out. But they were also,
with the same words, calling for the overthrow of a form of
government—specifically, the form of presidential dictatorship
that existed in most of the countries where the Arab spring had
the greatest impact.

One major consequence of the broader call for regime change
in this more general sense was to connect the different Arab
spring movements under a single structural rubric. To use the
same chant across multiple Arab states was to propose that all
were governed by the same regime, generically speaking. Despite

their individual differences, ran the implicit argument, the governments of Tunisia and Egypt and Syria and Libya and Yemen were all the same.

There was something true about this assertion. The dictatorial presidential republics that prevailed in several Arabic-speaking countries shared many significant features. They were (and are) not only instances of what Roger Owen called "Arab presidents for life"[15] but also structurally similar dictatorships built on complex and intricate combinations of military power, presidentially controlled secret services (*mukhabbarat*), and hybridized statist/market economics.

The regime commonalities suggested that Arab spring protesters in presidential dictatorships seemed to be objecting to the very form of government under which they were ruled. Support for this hypothesis may be gleaned from the subtly different rhetoric used by Arab spring protesters in the monarchies of Morocco and Jordan. In both countries, 2011 and after saw extensive public protests. But in both countries, protesters called for constitutional reform that would have changed the balance of power between the monarch and the government—not for the "overthrow of the regime."[16] If I am correct, the main reason for this difference is that Moroccans and Jordanians realistically sought change within the existing regime framework of constitutional monarchy—not the elimination of that form of government altogether. This might be because they did not think it was practically possible to overthrow their monarchs and feared retribution, because they perceived their monarchies as more legitimate than presidential dictatorships elsewhere, or a combination of the two. In any case, the difference was intentional.*

* It is noteworthy that in Bahrain, the mostly Shi'i protesters did call for the overthrow of the regime in the Sunni monarchy.

The protesters were also, at least in Tunisia, Egypt, Yemen, and Libya, hitting presidential dictatorship at its weakest point: the point of potential succession. In all four of those countries—the only four Arab states in which existing governments were replaced in the Arab spring—the presidential dictator was nearing the natural end of his career. Ben Ali was 74; Mubarak was 84; Ali Abdullah Saleh of Yemen was 70; Qaddafi was 68. All were in ill health.

Unlike monarchy and democracy, presidential dictatorship as a regime type has no definitive model for succession. Once in a great while a presidential dictator succeeds in passing power to a son. North Korea's regime has managed to do so twice, although the Communist structure of the DPRK makes the comparison inexact. In the Arab world, the only presidential dictator to pull off the succession trick was Hafez al-Assad. Saddam Hussein and Qaddafi would surely have tried; we will never know if they would have succeeded. Mubarak was clearly toying with the idea of trying to enable his son Gamal to succeed him, but Gamal lacked support from both the public and the army.

Seeking the overthrow of presidential dictatorships at the most vulnerable period in those regimes' life cycles helped propel the successes that the Arab spring achieved in its initial months. The prospect of transition vastly weakens individual dictators because regime participants need to ask themselves what will happen next. Instead of a clear prospect that continued loyalty to the regime will be rewarded with patronage and disloyalty with punishment, regime participants must consider that there may be no surviving entity capable of rewarding fealty and punishing dissent. The uncertainties of transition therefore lead institutional actors to try to calculate what might happen during and after regime change—and to try to pick the winning side in advance.

Under these conditions, not only the specific regimes but the regime type itself looked weak—especially once thousands of protesters went to the streets and would not leave. In essence, the protesters were daring the regime to put the protests down by force. To do so required the regimes to have the loyalty of enough state actors, whether police, intelligence services, or military, actually to achieve successful repression. That meant the state actors had to judge that it was in their continuing interests to support the regimes in actions that would be seen as opposing the interests of "the people." With transitions looming, some of the state actors began to balk. That created cracks in the regimes' facade of power that in turn left room for the possibility of regime change—or at least regime decapitation.

But if the regime type of presidential autocracy was to be overthrown, what was to replace it? Unspoken assumptions abounded, both within and outside the Arab spring countries. As is often the case when it comes to collective political action, the fact that the assumptions were unspoken allowed for coordinated action among people who might not otherwise have been able to agree if they spelled out their competing visions for what would follow. At the same time, the differences in the assumptions themselves sowed the seeds of future dissension among those who were coordinating on the short-term goal of regime overthrow.

Outside the Arabic-speaking world, it was mostly taken for granted that the Arab spring protesters wanted to replace their regimes with liberal, constitutional democracy. The main basis for this idea was the apparent political continuity of the Arab spring protests with the waves of constitutional democratization that followed the collapse of the Soviet Union. In the two decades between the fall of the Berlin wall and the Arab spring, it became a commonplace of global political discourse that peoples achieving freedom from various forms of autocratic or authoritarian government would voluntarily choose constitutional democracy as the only plausible and obvious alternative.

By 2011, it should also have been clear that the process of constitutional democratization was not simple or inevitable. Russia, for example, had long experienced major difficulties in democratizing, difficulties to a degree reminiscent of failed earlier waves of democratization in Europe and Latin America. Yet it is important to recall that 2011 was also well before the global crisis of constitutional democracy that came into focus around 2016. Populist right-wing governments had not yet begun to erode constitutional protections in Hungary and Poland. Turkey was still wrongly understood by many observers (myself included) as trending toward a greater degree of democracy. China's economic miracle had not yet begun to exert residual pressure on the appeal of constitutional democracy as a governmental model.

Within Arab spring countries, the nature of the unspoken assumptions about future directions was trickier to identify. On the one hand, it seems to have been generally assumed that the overthrow of regimes would be followed by elections. Those elections in turn were expected to choose representatives who would draft constitutions. The constitutional government in contemplation seems to have been democratic.

On the other hand, it is remarkable—and in retrospect highly noteworthy—that nowhere in the Arab spring protests did the term "democracy" figure as a major demand or desideratum. "Freedom, dignity, and social justice" was a common (rhymed) chant. Another, more economically oriented version called for "bread, freedom and social justice." Democracy could have been accommodated in either chant with only slight metrical adjustment and perfectly adequate rhyme. It was not.[17]

Why not? One conceivable answer is that the failure of U.S. efforts to replace Saddam Hussein's regime with constitutional democracy in Iraq had discredited the call for "democracy" as an effective rhetorical gambit among Arabic-speaking people. To demand democracy might have seemed naïve or, worse, might have seemed to play into a neoconservative account of how the Middle East needs to be democratized. On this view, democracy as a political slogan had been tarnished in the region by American imperialism and its distinctively incompetent efforts to effectuate its idealistic aspirations.

Of course, constitutional democracy might have continued to function as the default model of desirable government in the Arab spring countries even if it was not politically attractive to invoke that regime form as an aspiration. In this way, the embrace of constitutional democracy would not have been based on any inherent enthusiasm for it but simply on the Churchillian notion that it was the worst form of government except for all the others.

It is possible to reconcile the absence of a call for democracy with the default assumption of elections and constitution drafting in precisely this way. Indeed, one might even go a step further and say that the constitutional process in Iraq, covered in detail by Arabic-language satellite television, provided the default assumptions for what was supposed to happen in the aftermath of regime change. Thus, notwithstanding the failure of that process to create a fully satisfactory, legitimate government in Iraq, the Iraqi constitutional process came to shape background expectations.

Another possibility, of course, is that protesters avoided mentioning democracy not because it was especially tainted but because it was simply not what was motivating the protesters. In other words, the badness of the regime of presidential dictatorship wasn't that the dictators were not elected. It was that the

regimes systematically failed to provide freedom, dignity, or social justice.

This point of view is sometimes reflected by the observation,
or rather claim, that the moving force for the Arab spring protests was the breakdown of a "social contract" said to have legitimated the regimes that were being challenged.[18] According to
this interpretation, the presidential dictatorships long maintained
de facto legitimacy by delivering jobs, social welfare, and perhaps
national uplift. As they increasingly failed to deliver these public goods, tangible and intangible, they came to be challenged for
their illegitimacy.

I would like to push back against this interpretation. It is true
that "democracy" in the abstract was not a key stated demand of
the protesters. But I want to suggest that the "social contract"
imagined to have at one time legitimated the Arab dictatorships
is a chimera. The regime form of the Arab presidential dictatorships certainly did offer rhetorical justifications for its autocratic
nature. But it would be a serious mistake to confuse the regimes'
self-accountings for an implicit bargain between the public and
the government.

It might be argued that, in some sense, every regime not actively occupied in suppressing civil revolt operates on the basis
of a kind of social contract between the rulers and the ruled. On
this view, if the people are not actively rebelling, then they are
accepting the de facto legitimacy of the government. In turn, they
must be receiving some benefits—even if only the benefit of
avoiding anarchy.

Yet the term "social contract" implies, and ought to imply, a
form of political agreement substantially thicker than the mere
acceptance of oppressive rule as better than the alternative of
risky revolt. To say that Arab presidential dictatorships rested on
a social contract strongly implies that many citizens believed that

their governments were normatively legitimate, not merely that the dictator was managing to rule effectively. Normative legitimacy would mean that the public or some significant part of it accepted the ruler's authority or right to govern.

There is not sufficient evidence to support this implicit view of the pre–Arab spring presidential dictatorships. Certainly, there were constituencies in the relevant states that actively supported the regime—mostly because they benefited from that support. This would include the military as well as intelligence services and some sectors of the elite business community in Egypt, Tunisia, and Syria. But beyond the support of actors who judged that they were faring better under the dictatorship than they would have in its absence, there is no active reason to believe that the great majority of the public accepted the normative legitimacy of the dictatorships.[19]

The reason for this lack of evidence is that the dictatorships actively investigated, sought out, and punished political dissent. This authoritarian, autocratic mechanism, effectuated by the secret services, varied in degree from country to country. But in all the pre–Arab spring dictatorships, organized, sustained opposition to the state typically resulted in exile at best and incarceration and torture at worst. Opposition no doubt existed; but none of the countries had a legally recognized opposition movement with the capacity to express its views freely, much less appeal to the electorate.

Under these repressive conditions, it is difficult or impossible to imagine what evidence could convincingly prove the existence of a social contract in which the public actively embraced the regimes' normative legitimacy. Indeed, the state offered various public goods, including subsidies of basic foodstuffs, large sectors of state employment, low-cost education, and so forth. But to claim that these public goods bought normative legitimacy is just an assertion, not a claim based on observed or observable facts.

Rather, it is entirely possible, and indeed in my view highly probable, that most citizens of the presidential dictatorships took the public goods that were offered simply because they were offered, while withholding any active support for the dictatorships' normative legitimacy. Notice that I am not saying ordinary Tunisians, Egyptians, or Syrians were without national pride. Pride in the nation does not imply acceptance of the legitimacy of the regime controlling that nation's state. It is and was perfectly plausible for Egyptians to be proud of their culture and values without seeing the regime as the legitimate manifestation of Egyptian nationhood.

I am not speaking now of the 1950s and 1960s, when (I am prepared to believe) postcolonial Arab regimes may have possessed normative legitimacy intertwined with their emergence into independence and broadly socialist-nationalist ideology. I am arguing that the events of 2011 did not result from some sudden realization of a breached social contract that had been honored or enforced for the previous half century or so. Instead, that social contract had not existed for decades.

The interpretation I am offering posits that public dissatisfaction before the Arab spring was not great enough to motivate large numbers of people to take to the streets at great personal risk and demand the overthrow of the regime. Economic grievances including rising commodity prices, unemployment, and underemployment certainly played major roles in shifting public incentives. So did the aging of the dictators themselves. But the belief that the existing regimes were failing to deliver some combination of bread, freedom, dignity, and social justice did not suddenly emerge around the time of the Arab spring. It surely represented a long-developing feeling, one that did not so much erode the regimes' normative legitimacy as mark their ongoing illegitimacy.

The point of rejecting the putative breakdown of the hypothesized social contract is to help find an answer to the question of which type of regime the Arab spring protesters wanted to replace the one being overthrown. The answer, I think, is that the protesters did not have a clear idea of what that was. They were seeking a change in the structure of government that would provide economic and social justice—*without much specificity about what a new government would look like or how it would achieve those goals.*

Seen from this perspective, the reason the protesters did not call for democracy is not that they did not like it but simply that they were not focused on it. The protest was based on the absence of normatively legitimate government; the failure of the existing regime to produce jobs or dignity or social justice; and the sense that enough was enough. The protesters were not opposed to the idea that democracy might provide solutions to these failures and absences. But they did not express, and in many instances very probably did not hold, the a priori view that the lack of democracy was the essence of their regimes' problem or that democracy was the definitive solution.

As I shall argue later, the protesters' uncertainty about the relationship between democracy and the social changes that they sought has led to fascinating and strange consequences in Tunisia. There, the greatest consequence of the Arab spring is that constitutional democracy is taking hold. Yet the problems of economic opportunity and social justice remain as unsolved as under Ben Ali. And if constitutional rights confer dignity on some persons, they are not on their own usually sufficient to effect a transformation in the society's self-conception.

For now, it is enough to say that the wish for the overthrow of the regime was a wish for its replacement by some better regime—some type or form of government that would better serve the values of dignity and social justice and the closely related material aspiration for jobs. In Egypt, that aspiration went awry as elections led to a new government and regime that in turn gave way to a new presidential dictatorship eerily similar to the old one. In Syria, the result was even worse than this structure of recurrence. The aspiration to overthrow the regime led to a civil war fought by the regime to avoid its overthrow. That led to years of anarchy, mass destruction, mass migration, and mass deaths—all of which ended in the survival of the regime.

Conclusion: The People and the Call to Collective Action

By exploring the political meanings of the call by "the people" to overthrow their regimes, I have, I hope, also elucidated the beginnings of a theory of autonomous collective action in the Arab spring (my first major argument) and its relation to Arab nationalism (the focus of my second major argument). Whether the peoples were national or transnational, the pan-Arab character and transnational Arabic linguistic forms of the demand for action called into being a movement that sought *self*-determination. The next steps may have been uncertain, and the precise identity of who would do the work of overthrow was underspecified. But the political character of the demand was not uncertain at all. It was a demand for change made by the people, on behalf of the people, and insisting therefore on the people's right to make that change. The demands did not implicate imperial powers but Arabs—Arab peoples and Arab leaders.

Before the Arab spring began to go awry, then, its protesters deployed an implicit image of the Arab (pan-)nation, connected across geography, language, and culture. The constituent peoples of the broader nation were rising, not precisely together but also not precisely separately. They wanted or willed some transformation in the nature of the regime forms that many shared in common. In the next chapter, we shall explore the difficult meaning of what happened when the most populous Arab nation-state actually did change its regime form—then reconsidered the decision in a second, revanchist round of collective political action.

CHAPTER 2

TAHRIR AND THE PROBLEM OF AGENCY

Agency

Having begun by exploring (albeit in stylized form) the content of the Arab spring protesters' aspirations, I turn now to the normative significance of the protests' political consequences. In answering these questions, I will focus on Egypt, using Tahrir Square as a representative symbol of the possibility and meaning of collective political action. The question I want to ask is: Did the people speak in Tahrir? And if they did, why and how does that matter?

Tahrir is particularly instructive because it was the symbolic-geographical focal point of two distinct moments of collective political action, each taken by protesters claiming to act on behalf of the Egyptian people. For convenience, those two moments can be described by the dates used by many protesters to name them: the January 25 movement or revolution, referring to the date of the first mass protests against Hosni Mubarak in Tahrir in 2011; and the June 30 movement or revolution, referring to the date of the first mass protests against Mohamed Morsi in 2013.

My central argument can be stated simply. If you believe that the Egyptian people acted through the January 25 revolution to replace Mubarak, the dictator, then you should also believe that the Egyptian people acted through the June 30 revolution to replace Morsi, the democratically elected president. The Egyptian people acted as agents of their own political future by calling for the overthrow of the regime. Then the Egyptian people acted as agents of their own political future by overthrowing the regime that had replaced it—effectively inviting the return of the very regime they had overthrown two and a half years before.

Consequently, Egypt's authoritarian presidential dictatorship was not the product of the people's will before 2011. But Egypt's authoritarian presidential dictatorship is today, in the aftermath of the June 30 revolution, the product of the people's will. The people acted; and they acted mistakenly. They took their fate in their hands—and gave it away.

If you can, before you launch mental countermeasures in rejection of this rather stark claim, pause to let me lay out its component parts.

The first, and unquestionably the most important, is the notion of agency. I would like to define agency here as the conscious, intentional choice of a person or group to act in ways that determine the outcome of relevant political events. Much like the related concept of popular "will," agency can be analyzed as a matter of historical sociology or as a matter of normative political theory.

My definition encompasses elements of both historical agency and political agency. I am primarily interested in the evaluative side, in the orbit of political theory. Yet to get to a plausible normative vision, I need some rudimentary account of historical action. It is not enough for me that people are *trying* to determine the outcome of events relevant to them. To be agents, people must actually *be* determining the outcome of events, to the extent it is possible to speak coherently about determination when it comes to history.

To say that a person or a people are historical agents is ordinarily to say that they are determining the course of relevant events themselves, rather than having that course of events determined for them by outside forces. A historical agent is sometimes said to be a "subject" of action, rather than an "object" of it.

As the philosophical nature of the terms "subject" and "object" suggests, they are redolent of political theory more than of concrete history. But they do capture the basic historical intuition that some people are actors or active agents in the making of history while others are recipients or sufferers or victims—not necessarily passive victims but in any case unable to take effective action to determine outcomes. Historical agents in this sense are people making their own history.

Of course, no one makes history in isolation. A mosaic of people and groups contribute to outcomes, as do structural forces like economics, politics, technology, and climate. Power itself is composed of multiple elements that always include opposed forces. Thus, to be a historical agent cannot mean that the agent *alone* shapes relevant outcomes. The judgment must be relative: a historical agent is, thus, one who contributes to relevant historical outcomes more than other actors and more, measured somehow or other, than impersonal forces of history.

From this compressed account of historical agency, it should be clear that from some historical points of view, there can never be any such thing as a historical agent. Some historians believe that it would be impossible to gauge plausibly the relative contributions of different actors to any given historical event. Others think historical causality has too many moving parts to attribute agency to any one or more causes. Still others believe that structural factors, not individuals or groups of people, determine historical outcomes. According to this last view, human historical agency is a phantom phenomenon based on our tendency to overstate conscious individuals' intentional contribution to events.

I have no desire here to refute these various entirely plausible critiques of historical agency. But I do want to note that if any of these is ultimately correct, then there can be no coherent account of *political* agency that in any way rests on the effectiveness of agents' intentional political action. To have a theory of political agency in which we can say that the people have acted as agents (or that a subgroup of people have legitimately acted as agents on their behalf), we first need to accept, in some rudimentary form, the possibility that people or groups of people can act as agents in history.

For reasons of parsimony, I would much prefer to be able to make an argument for political agency without relying on some prior necessary version of historical agency. I would love to be able to claim, for example, that the Egyptian people acted as agents in the January 25 revolution, without having to take any view about whether the fall of Mubarak was in fact determined in some important degree by the Tahrir protesters. That would spare me from having to consider the extremely difficult historical question of what brought down the regime. And it would enable me to ascribe political agency to the Egyptian people even if, on the best historical account, they did not determine the overthrow.

But I find that I cannot do without historical agency because it seems so crucial that political agency not be a mere fantasy. If a group of people who claimed to act on behalf of "the people" believed that their actions enabled the overthrow of Mubarak, but they were wrong in that belief, I do not see how they could be said to have exercised political agency. Rather, such people might hold the deluded belief that they acted as political agents, without in fact having done so.

Agents of History

To advance my argument about the two Tahrir-focused movements, then, I first need to convince you that the protesters played a determinative role in bringing down the Mubarak regime. That is, the protesters had a greater role in ending the regime than, say, the Egyptian military (an internal actor); the United States (an external actor); or structural features of the political-economic situation.

To be clear, I mean to acknowledge that the army, not the protesters, removed Mubarak. On the evening of February 10, 2011, Mubarak addressed the nation and announced that he would not step down until after elections the following September.[1] On February 11, Omar Suleiman, Egypt's vice president, delivered a one-sentence address to the effect that Mubarak was stepping down and transferring power to the Supreme Council of the Armed Forces.[2] Nothing had changed overnight except that the military had dictated its decision to the president.

But I want to argue that the army could not and would not have taken this step without the protests. That is, the action of the protesters was the factor that, more than any other, caused the military to remove Mubarak. The popular protesters were therefore the historical agents of Mubarak's removal.

One very strong reason to think that the Egyptian army would not have removed Mubarak but for the Tahrir protests is that, before the protests, the army made no visible effort to do so.

There were some independent reasons that the military might have had for acting. Mubarak was perceived to be positioning his son Gamal as a potential successor, and the military had no love for Gamal. The problem of transition loomed as Mubarak aged. But had the military taken unilateral action to remove the president and replace him, its actions would not have been perceived as legitimate by most Egyptians. Encouraging instability through a coup d'état would have been highly risky. The best strategy for the military, even assuming it did not want to accept Gamal as Mubarak's successor, was to wait for Mubarak's death and then try to block Gamal from becoming president.

The Tahrir protests changed the military's calculus in a fundamental way. The protests told the military that support of Mubarak or inaction would both have potentially major costs for its institutional standing. Large numbers of people were publicly calling for the overthrow of the regime. The military certainly understood that it could be construed as the addressee of this request. It was, after all, the only institution in the country capable of effecting the removal unless Mubarak stepped down voluntarily—which seemed unlikely given his experience, character, and plans for his son. Instability was growing daily. If the military actively aided Mubarak, it would be condemned by the same protesters who were condemning the president. If it remained neutral, the military ran the risk of being perceived as too weak to act. If and when the regime were to fall, it would be perceived as having fallen despite the military's inaction.

The protests furthermore showed the military that it had much to gain from removing Mubarak. The greatest prize was massive institutional legitimacy. If the army appeared to be acting at the behest of the people, it would consolidate the belief that the army was uniquely the only institution in the country that was serving the people's interests. From this perspective, it did not much matter whether the call for the overthrow of the regime was directed at the military. It was sufficient that the military could treat the protesters' call as though it had been addressed to it.

Another great advantage the military could gain from removing Mubarak was ensuring that succession would not pass to Gamal. The president's son had tried over the years to develop a power base that would enable him to assume the presidency and then govern without having to rely disproportionally on the military. His core strategy was to empower a new entrepreneurial elite that would be committed to economic development and personally loyal to him. Yet because the Egyptian military is also a significant actor in the Egyptian economy, this put Gamal's strategy into conflict with the military's business interests. Not only was the military threatened by the possibility of quasi-liberalizing economic reforms. It could also see clearly that if Gamal succeeded, the military's long-term position as the most powerful institution in the country could ultimately be supplanted.

The reciprocal advantage of blocking Gamal's road to the presidency was for the military to influence who would in fact be chosen. It is not known—and perhaps not knowable—whether the military contemplated fully free democratic elections. On the face of it, that seems unlikely. But the military must have predicted that, through exercising influence on the Egyptian constitutional court (the judicial body with supervisory power over elections), it could at least shape the field of presidential candidates.

A complicating twist was that the military must also have realized that if elections were held, the Muslim Brotherhood would seek to contest them. Again, it is not known at present whether the army already had a coherent strategy for confronting or co-opting the Brotherhood; in view of later events, it seems most likely that it did not. The Brotherhood may also have made pledges to the military not to seek to control the legislature or the presidency, pledges they did not keep. Regardless, the military leadership must have calculated that the risks associated with the potential electoral rise of the Brotherhood were outweighed by the dangers of inaction and the benefits of removing Mubarak. The protests were what made the definitive difference.

Agents of Political Freedom

If I have convinced you that the protests in Tahrir were the key *historical* causal factor that led the army to remove Mubarak, that brings us to the question of *political* agency. The question I am now asking is, in essence: Did "the people" act in Tahrir? That is, were the protests that led to Mubarak's removal a legitimate expression of the will of the Egyptian people to take charge of their own fate in the realm of politics?

To this question my answer is a resounding yes. The people who were actually in Tahrir, claiming to act and speak on behalf of the abstraction "the people," were in fact contributing directly to throwing off tyranny. They were participating in the ultimate political act of shaping their own governmental regime in accordance with what the majority of Egyptians would eventually choose it to be. The people's action was politically legitimate. More than that, it was noble—noble in the sense that one of the highest aspirations of humanity is and should be engaging in the capacity to self-govern and determine the collective political future. The reaction around the Arabic-speaking world and beyond to the spectacle of tyranny removed at the apparent behest of an engaged public reflected the belief that political freedom is a worthy and worthwhile way of being in the world.

Of course, I do not mean to suggest that everyone, and certainly not every Egyptian, would have shared the same sense of elation.* Those personally close to the Mubarak regime must have felt foreboding and fear. Minorities like Egyptian Copts who relied on the regime's protection might have felt, entirely reasonably, that a popular uprising unmoored from the existing political order boded ill for them. Supporters of Israel living outside Egypt might (also reasonably) have feared that a popularly elected Egyptian government would be far less inclined toward preserving the peace with Israel than an autocracy dependent on conditional U.S. military aid. There must also have been some true antidemocrats out there in the world watching, people who believe that self-government is a dangerous delusion that leads to trouble.

Yet I would wager that even most of those who did not feel unmitigated joy at the prospect of the popular defeat of tyranny did feel *some* twinge of connection or pride or human pleasure when Mubarak fell. That twinge, however repressed by competing feelings of fear or self-interest, represents the flicker of the ideal of political self-determination. That ideal is powerful—not only in the West but anywhere on earth where ideas of political freedom have reached, which is almost everywhere.

I am not here offering a detailed argument about why free political action is a crucial component of human flourishing. That argument has been made by philosophers from Aristotle to

---

* A March–April 2011 Gallup poll suggested that 83 percent of Egyptians then supported the revolution. Gallup, "Egypt from Tahrir to Transition," https://news.gallup.com/poll/157046/egypt-tahrir-transition.aspx. Similar results were obtained by other contemporaneous polls; see International Republican Institute, April 2011, http://www.iri.org/sites/default/files/2011%20June%205%20Survey%20of%20Egyptian%20Public%20Opinion,%20April%2014–27,%202011_0.pdf (82 percent of Egyptians strongly approved of the events that led to Mubarak's resignation).

named for the British and French diplomats who did the deal, was the enduring symbol of this imperial division. The temporary breakdown of the Syria-Iraq border at the hands of the Islamic State after the Arab spring, to which we will return when discussing Syria and Iraq, was presented by the Islamic State and treated by others as a symbol of the eventual passing of the borders that emerged from the imperial era.[4] Finally came the United States and the Soviet Union, which themselves took different Arabic-speaking countries as their allies and proxies. When the Soviet Union collapsed, the United States became the sole imperial actor in the region for a quarter century. It took the civil war in Syria, we shall see, for Russia to reemerge as an important, if post-imperial, actor.

I want to suggest that the political agency exercised by Arab peoples in the Arab spring was importantly connected to the decline of empire in the region—especially the failure and retreat of the U.S. imperial presence in the decade of the 2000s. That is, I want to offer a geopolitical account of the emergence of political self-determination. I am not arguing that it was U.S. decline that primarily caused the Arab spring. Rather, I am arguing that the weakening of empire was an important condition in setting the circumstances for self-determination to emerge.

The imperial decline I am describing was itself caused by various forces, including the financial crisis of 2007–8. But the most proximate cause for the decline of U.S. imperial power in the Arabic-speaking world was the overstretch embodied by the failure of the U.S. invasion of Iraq. To be more precise, the cause of decline lay in the failure of the postwar occupation of Iraq, which both revealed the limits of U.S. capacity in the region and discouraged the American public from contemplating any repetition of the effort.

A full analysis of the regional and global meaning of U.S. involvement in Iraq remains still to be written, and this is not the place for it. But it is necessary and I hope valuable here to offer a brief preview of what such an account might look like—because the events in Iraq from 2003 to 2011 provide a crucial background for understanding the Arab spring and its aftermath from 2011 to the present.

The identifiable historical framework for understanding U.S. efforts in the Middle East is that of imperial overstretch. Consider that the U.S. "empire" in the region before 2003 took a markedly different form from that of traditional imperial powers. The United States funded and provided military support for close allies including Israel, Egypt, and Saudi Arabia. It supported one of those states, Israel, in its proxy war against Soviet ally Syria in the early 1980s. Yet in the entire Cold War period, in which the United States fought two large land wars in Asia and several smaller ones in Latin America, the United States never invaded a Middle Eastern state.*

As the Soviet Union declined, the United States fought a single war in the Arabic-speaking world: the Gulf War of 1991 to remove the forces of Saddam Hussein's Iraq from Kuwait. In that limited, six-week engagement, the administration of George H. W. Bush spent five weeks bombarding ostensibly military targets in Iraq and Kuwait from the air. It then sent a large ground force to displace the Iraqi troops, an operation that lasted less than a week and resulted in the destruction of a significant part of Saddam's fleeing army. The first Bush administration famously chose not to march on Baghdad, which was largely

---

* With the arguable exception of the U.S. marine landing in Beirut in July 1958, intended to support Lebanese president Camille Chamoun by controlling the sea and air ports to the city. U.S. ships and troops withdrew in October 1958.

undefended, or to attempt to remove Saddam from office. The administration judged that Saddam was a useful regional counterweight to Iran and feared the practical consequences of regime change.

The self-imposed limits of the first Gulf War reflected a strategic vision of the cautious use of imperial power. Having pursued its first ground war in the Middle East to a successful conclusion, the Bush administration believed it had effectively sent the message that the United States could and would intercede at will in the region to impose its preferred order. This was undoubtedly an imperial view, but it was an imperial view that sought to avoid lengthy entanglement that would be reminiscent of the U.S. experience in Vietnam. The administration of Bill Clinton maintained a similar posture. It sanctioned Saddam and maintained a no-fly zone that gave de facto autonomy to the Kurdish region in northern Iraq. But it did not contemplate a full-on invasion or occupation of the country.

After the September 11 attacks, the administration of George W. Bush abandoned the restraint of its two predecessors. The initially successful invasion of Afghanistan, which quickly displaced the Taliban, gave the administration confidence that the United States could defeat Saddam with a far lighter force than had been deployed in the Gulf War. That turned out to be correct. A ground force of fewer than 100,000 troops—perhaps a fifth or sixth of those deployed in 1990–91—brought down Saddam Hussein's regime in just a few weeks in March–April 2003.

The overstretch began right away. The remarkably small size of the force was intended in part to ensure the United States would avoid the temptation of a lengthy occupation. Secretary of Defense Donald Rumsfeld wanted a military that could be deployed nimbly to achieve strategic objectives without becoming bogged down in Vietnam-style combat. Yet as it turned out, the very lightness of the force rendered it incapable of establishing effective order in occupied Iraq. To make matters worse, the United States disbanded the Iraqi military and police, leaving no effective sovereign at all. After a brief lull during which regime elements and ordinary Iraqis sought to make sense of how the United States intended to operate, there commenced a slow but steadily growing Sunni insurgency that threatened the stability of the postwar order that the United States hoped to establish.

In a desperate attempt to replace the eliminated state apparatus, the United States established a nominally sovereign Iraqi government while continuing de facto occupation. This effort, once begun, left the occupier with little choice but to remain in Iraq and engage in an extended effort at state reconstruction. This was, and is, a textbook example of imperial overstretch: undertaking an expensive, dangerous, time-consuming task for which the empire is ill-suited as the unintended result of the expression of imperial power. Its consequences in Iraq are well known. By 2011, extensive counterinsurgency efforts (the U.S. military "surge," initiated in 2007) had temporarily put down the Sunni insurgency. The surge established the rule, if not the authority, of a coalition government in Baghdad made up of Shi'i and Kurdish parties who had promised a greater share of power to Sunni Arabs as part of the political effort to put down the insurgency.

The effect of the overstretch was twofold. Within the United States, the Iraq experience—combined with what turned out to be a still less successful experience in Afghanistan—soured the American public on lengthy, engaged intervention in the Middle East or elsewhere in the Islamic world. True, the Obama administration participated in the bombing campaign that removed Muammar al-Qaddafi from office and cast Libya into its own civil war. Eventually, the United States also began a bombing campaign in Syria. But there was no domestically viable option of putting U.S. ground troops in combat anywhere in the countries affected by the Arab spring (at least not until the rise of the Islamic State in 2014, and even then in relatively small numbers). From the standpoint of domestic U.S. politics, overstretch was met with retrenchment and retraction.

The other, corresponding effect of the American imperial overstretch in Iraq was expressed regionally. The United States would take no major steps to either effectuate or promote the events of the Arab spring. Instead, the Obama administration adopted a position of cautiously seeking to maintain a middle ground from which, Obama hoped, he would not be criticized either for crushing the hopes of self-empowered Arabs or for creating circumstances of regime collapse that led to civil war.

In the case of Syria, this middle-ground policy ended up having enormous, highly visible consequences, which I will explore later. In Egypt, the consequences were less clear but perhaps not less significant. Specifically, the Tahrir protesters soon discovered that while they would not receive active support from the United States, neither would the United States intervene actively in support of the Mubarak regime. This compromise position was well expressed by a highly publicized phone call that Obama made to Mubarak on February 2, 2011. In the call, Obama said that transition in Egypt "must begin now."[5] Since Mubarak had already announced that he would not seek office in elections the following September, Obama's carefully calibrated position was intended to encourage visible public progress toward transition without signaling that the United States was demanding Mubarak's ouster.

The ambivalence of the U.S. signal made sense in the context of its imperial overstretch and subsequent retrenchment. What this signaled to Egyptians was that the Obama administration was going to try to let the Arab spring play out on its own, without taking a determinative role. This position was not at all characteristic of a classic imperial actor, one that tries (as the United States had done in Iraq) to dictate outcomes and specify regimes. Rather, it reflected the limits of an imperial power exhausted and discouraged by its failure to pick winners and establish democracy in an Arabic-speaking country.

The upshot of this U.S. position was to open the door for the exercise of political agency by Egyptians and other Arab spring actors. Where in the past, political agency had been thwarted by imperial imposition, now the retreating empire was prepared to tolerate the exercise of independent agency—not because it wanted to but because it felt it had few alternatives. In this limited sense, the invasion of Iraq and its aftermath contributed to the acts of political agency that characterized the Arab spring.

The American stance also had very substantial practical consequences for the way events unfolded in Egypt. The fact that the United States was not going to try to choose a winner meant that any of the various political actors who sought power and control in the aftermath of Mubarak's departure had a chance of winning. The United States was prepared to work with and even recognize the Supreme Council of the Armed Forces (SCAF), the body that sat at the top of the military. It was willing to recognize and work with the Muslim Brotherhood–led government of Mohamed Morsi. And ultimately, the United States was willing to recognize and work with the government of Abdel Fattah el-Sisi after the army brought down Morsi. That is, the intervention of the weakened American empire would not get in the way of the political agency of Egyptians in determining the outcome of the two-year struggle over political power.

The Road to Tahrir II

The complex events in the period between Mubarak's removal on February 11, 2011, and the removal of Morsi on July 3, 2013, deserve their own book-length historical treatment to supplement early efforts by journalists. Since detailed, archive-based scholarly accounts are not yet available, I will offer here a tentative interpretation of the events. The point of my account is not to document every twist and turn in this highly dramatic period but to set the stage for a second argument about political agency: that the Tahrir protests that led to the army's removal of Morsi were manifestations of collective political agency every bit as much as were the protests that led to the removal of Mubarak.

I want to emphasize and acknowledge that a meaningful portion of the Egyptian population did not want to see the democratically elected president removed from office. By the middle of June 2013, 29 percent of Egyptians reported confidence in Morsi.[6] Thus almost a third of Egyptians wanted Morsi to remain in office. As for the others, a lack of confidence in the president is not necessarily the same as a desire to see him removed by force. It is thus conceivable that more than a third of Egyptians opposed Morsi's ouster.[7]

I also want to state clearly that, as a normative matter, I myself rejected and still reject the army's coup as an illegitimate usurpation of the democratic process. Nevertheless, what is at issue is not my view or preference but the political agency of the people who went to Tahrir and facilitated Morsi's ouster in much the same manner as people had gone to the square to enable the removal of Mubarak. As I shall argue, this exercise of political agency was a historic, generational mistake—but it was nevertheless a legitimate expression of collective political agency.

The essence of my reading of events in Egypt from the spring of 2011 to the summer of 2013 is that the army and the Muslim Brotherhood were engaged in an intricate, iterative process of bilateral bargaining, bluffing, and encounter. Often their dance resembled a tango: passionate, forceful, with violence barely suppressed and sometimes erupting fully. And the tango carried with it at all times the possibility that one dancer would try to stab the other in the heart.[8]

In brief, the choreography went like this: From the start, the SCAF recognized that the only large, organized institutional entity in the country capable of contesting elections was the Brotherhood. Also from the start, the Brotherhood leadership understood that the military had the capacity to suppress it and exclude its members from power altogether. Each sought to accommodate the other temporarily, while each sought ultimate victory in a struggle for political authority and legitimacy.

After Mubarak stepped down on February 11, the SCAF was open to the possibility that it might not have to hold free elections at all, and it sought to delay the democratic process. The idea would have been for the SCAF to govern directly by popular consensus until a tame presidential candidate could be fielded. Further public protests, which reignited on February 25, signaled that this was not realistic. In particular, the Brotherhood, which had been a late entrant into the Tahrir protests, made its presence and numbers felt through public demonstrations that signaled to the army it would have to allow elections—in which the Brotherhood would be free to compete openly, for the first time in the party's history in Egypt.

The SCAF nonetheless sought to limit the Brotherhood's impact by pressuring the Presidential Election Commission, a body of senior judges it appointed, to block the candidacies of the Brotherhood leaders most likely to be elected.[9] These included Khairat el-Shater, the Brotherhood's well-known deputy supreme guide. (The SCAF also had the longtime head of intelligence Omar Suleiman blocked from running—presumably in order to maintain the appearance of impartiality.) The SCAF clearly hoped that it could block the Brotherhood from winning the presidency at all.

After considerable internal debate and division, the Brotherhood responded by running Mohamed Morsi, a senior, conservative Brotherhood figure who had not been expected to emerge as a presidential hopeful and was parodied as the movement's "spare tire."[10] In this important sense, Morsi was an accidental candidate, deemed by the SCAF to be weak enough to be acceptable given the constraint of having to allow *someone* from the Brotherhood orbit to run. The squabbles within the Brotherhood also had the effect of weakening Morsi's ties to the rest of the Brotherhood's leadership, which inevitably wondered why he had been allowed to run and they had not.

The popular elections for president, held in two rounds, revealed that the public slightly preferred a Brotherhood candidate, even one who was relatively unknown, to a candidate seen as closer to the SCAF and the old regime. In the first round, Morsi won 24.8 percent of the votes. In the second round, he more than doubled that result, winning 51.7 percent of the votes and defeating Ahmad Shafiq, Mubarak's last prime minister and a former air force general, who won 48.3 percent.[11] This was far from being a ringing endorsement of Morsi or the Brotherhood. It suggested that the public chose Morsi over Shafiq as a relative preference among the candidates available. At the same time, it also showed the military that the Brotherhood was not going to be defeated easily. It had combined a first-mover advantage, common to Islamist parties in Arabic-speaking countries when free elections were first held, with a strong anti-statist stance. To vote for Morsi was to vote for change.

In the year that followed Morsi's inauguration, both the Brotherhood and the military continued their struggle against one another. The army's biggest success, achieved via the constitutional court, was the disbanding of the democratically elected parliament, in which the Brotherhood would have enjoyed a slight majority.[12] This left Morsi isolated and essentially guaranteed that he could only rule by decree—which weakened his claim to democratic legitimacy.

Morsi's greatest victory in this period—a rather stunning one, in retrospect—was a purge of the senior ranks of the military, including major SCAF figures like Field Marshal Mohamed Hussein Tantawi. It is little short of amazing that, despite the institutional power of the military, an elected president could bully general officers into retirement with the threat of prosecution and pull it off without provoking an immediate coup d'état. Elements of the military must have cooperated in the retirement scheme for it to work. In any case, the accomplishment is a testament to the democratic legitimacy that Morsi enjoyed, however temporarily. It is also a testament to the tactical brilliance of the younger general who replaced Tantawi and played a major role in keeping the army in line during the change in senior leadership: Abdel Fattah el-Sisi.[13]

The fact is that Morsi chose or at least accepted the military's choice of Sisi as his commander in chief—and hence, perhaps unwittingly, as his adversary and nemesis. To be sure, Morsi had to accept one of a handful of general officers who were young enough not to be part of the SCAF inner circle, while also well connected and experienced enough to become credible leaders. Sisi headed military intelligence and therefore had a position of importance within the SCAF. Morsi's choice of Sisi was thus not unconstrained. But it was a choice nonetheless, perhaps the most fateful of the entire Arab spring in Egypt. Indeed, one way to think of the personalities involved in the Egyptian drama is that the SCAF was fortunate in having Morsi as its opponent—while Morsi was unfortunate in getting Sisi.

Morsi's choice of Sisi, if that is what it was, has been pondered and will deserve further pondering by future historians who are able to understand his range of options better. For now, it is enough to note that many observers thought Morsi was comfortable with Sisi because of the latter's projection of traditional religiosity in his personal life. Unlike the wives of many senior generals, Sisi's wife, Entissar Amer, covered her hair with a hijab.[14] Sisi also prayed regularly and cultivated the subtle forehead callus that publicized that fact.[15] This sort of public piety would have been rare among the older generation of general officers, whose careers had overlapped more fully with the Mubarak regime.

That older generation never forgot that Mubarak had come to power after a religious zealot—whom today we would call a jihadi—assassinated Anwar el-Sadat on the basis of a religious justification. The pragmatic religion of the Brotherhood was drastically different from the ideological extremism of Sadat's assassin. But the cultural divide between Egyptians who take their religion seriously and those who wear it lightly remained, especially among the governing elite. Morsi seems to have viewed Sisi as belonging to his side of the divide.

The most salient proof that Morsi got Sisi wrong is that after Sisi's elevation, the army did not change its stance toward the Brotherhood or the elected Morsi government. Efforts to direct the constitutional court continued apace, as we shall soon see. More broadly, the military gave no sign of opposing the resistance to Morsi that never ceased to emanate from the bureaucratic remnants of the Mubarak regime.

Frequently, the term "deep state" has been used to characterize the bureaucratic resistance to Morsi's government. Although the term has no precise definition, and has been distorted by its subsequent adoption into the U.S. political sphere by Donald Trump, it is typically used to describe entrenched career civil servants, especially those employed in security and intelligence services, who exercise power that is not easily limited or redirected by a new government, elected or otherwise. Since all modern governments feature a career civil service that is *supposed* to act apolitically, the notion of the "deep state" must be intended to describe the *overreach* of those bureaucrats, particularly efforts they might undertake to work against the interests of the new government and its policies.

In Egypt, at least, the "deep state" is said by some to have deliberately slowed delivery of basic state services including energy, trash collection, and even food subsidies in order to make the Morsi government seem ineffective. The allegation here is one of intentional sabotage. As for the security and intelligence services, they are said to have, at a minimum, weakened their surveillance of radical elements in order to enable or even encourage terrorist attacks.

I cannot judge the accuracy of any of these accounts, although all sound possible. For my purposes, it is enough to say that the role of the "deep state" in weakening the Morsi government, if any, was perfectly consistent with the demonstrated efforts of the army to do the same. This in turn is perfectly consistent with the intuition that former old regime participants wanted, if possible, to turn back the clock by weakening Morsi and eventually replacing him. The deck was stacked against Morsi from the beginning.

That reality does not, in my view, detract from the many serious errors that Morsi and the Brotherhood made along the way to his removal from office, his arrest, and the violent suppression of the Brotherhood—not to mention errors made by the rest of democratic civil society. Notwithstanding the long odds, however, Morsi did have a *chance* of consolidating democracy. To do so, he would have had to compromise extensively on principles, as well as on power sharing.

The playbook for how to achieve such compromise was not obscure or unavailable. As we shall see in chapter 5, it was being composed in real time in Tunisia. Indeed, senior ranking members of the Tunisian Ennahda Party, itself originally an offshoot of the Brotherhood, were initially consulted by Morsi. Rached el-Ghannouchi, the leader of Ennahda, flew repeatedly to Egypt to give advice and in June 2012 even addressed a rally in Tahrir Square alongside Morsi.[16] Yet for the most part, the Brotherhood did not listen to Ennahda's counsel of compromise or imitate its model of backing away from what had once been seen as core Islamist political demands.

The Egyptian Brotherhood's reasons for refusing to compromise broadly and share power extensively had two distinct bases. One was a majoritarian misconception of democracy. Morsi seemed to be under the mistaken impression that, having won slim electoral majorities, the Brotherhood was entitled to govern essentially on its own. That is rarely how democracy works in practice. In almost any democratic situation, but especially in the processes of government formation and constitution drafting, substantial electoral minorities must be incorporated and accommodated. If not, electoral losers will judge that they have no stake in the emerging governing structure—and will seek to undermine democracy rather than sustain it.

Hence, the most fundamental lesson of constitution making is that meaningful electoral minorities must inevitably be given more than their fair share of say in the system. That is the price of doing business in a constitutional democracy. Potential spoilers set the price through their implicit—and sometimes explicit—threat to sink the entire government and process. This lesson can be observed in constitution-making processes from Philadelphia in 1787 to Baghdad in 2004. The Tunisian Ghannouchi emphasized it in another Cairo speech in June 2013, when he urged against "democracy of the majority" and said that the alternative to accepting societal diversity would be "conflict or chaos."[17]

Morsi ignored the lesson. By failing to accommodate, co-opt, buy out, or otherwise empower those who had lost at the ballot box, he deepened already existing incentives for them to block Egyptian democracy from emerging. In this way, Morsi almost invited the crisis that built against him and the subsequent restoration of military government. This willful ignorance, also reflected in Morsi's apparent lack of interest in consultation with outsiders regarding the constitutional process, had massive consequences.

Morsi's other error had to do with paranoia. He and the Brotherhood assumed that, in the same way that the military and the deep state sought to bring down his government, liberal secularists who criticized his government also sought his demise. For this reason, he did not seek out potential liberal, secularist allies to participate in his government. Furthermore, he may have believed that even an alliance with liberal secularists would not be able to save him from the army if it chose to remove him.

As the old saw has it, even paranoids have enemies. Morsi was not wrong to see conspiracies all around him. The Egyptian elites were full of people who wished for nothing more than the downfall of the Brotherhood government. Undoubtedly, some or even many liberal secularists were so unsympathetic to the Brotherhood's Islamist politics, and so worried about the further

Islamization of the Egyptian state and society, that they were willing to sell out what democratic impulses they had and side with the army.

Yet Morsi's decision not to reach out to liberal secularists was nevertheless a historic error. Ultimately, the vocal presence of liberal secularists in the events that delegitimized Morsi's government and helped open the door to the second coup d'état. Had the liberal secularists been inside Morsi's government, not outside, they might not have alone been able to block a military takeover. But their presence would have made the military takeover much more difficult—because they would have been visible symbols of the democratic character of the elected Morsi government. And they might not have played such a central role in bringing Morsi down in the second wave of protests.

Had Morsi and the Brotherhood shared power rather than going it alone, they still might not have survived. But their odds of survival would have been far greater. Instead, by the fall of 2012, just a few months after Morsi was elected in June, his government found itself in the grips of a legitimacy crisis. It is to this crisis that we must now turn—one created by the constitutional court under the influence of the military, and then exploited and highlighted by the eventual emergence of the so-called June 30 movement: the popular movement designed in imitation of the January 25 movement and that intended to call on the army to topple the democratically elected Morsi presidency.

Agency Redux

As the events in Egypt were unfolding, it did not seem that the June 30 movement that sought the removal of Mohamed Morsi deserved the same sort of political legitimacy as the

January 25 movement that sought the overthrow of Mubarak. After all, Mubarak was a tyrant, and the aspiration to remove him was grounded, as I have argued, in a basic desire by Egyptians for the people to take charge of their fate and act freely. In contrast, Morsi was a democratically elected president.

True, Morsi and his party had made serious missteps in their brief time trying to exercise government. They had drafted a constitution in great haste, forcing the resulting document through the drafting body. Morsi himself had issued a controversial declaration blocking the constitutional court from removing him from office until the constitution was ratified. And whether because of incompetence or institutional opponents blocking his moves, Morsi's government had done a poor job of delivering basic services.

Yet in my view, then and now, these mistakes did not obviate Morsi's claim to be the democratically legitimate president of Egypt. Each of several times that the public was allowed to vote in the post–Arab spring period, the results favored Morsi and the Muslim Brotherhood, even if their majority was slim and declining as participation also went down. Morsi had been elected in a free election. His political party had won a plurality in national assembly elections. The constitution, drafted under pressure in the worst possible circumstances, had nevertheless subsequently been ratified in a popular referendum.

As for the charge that Morsi was governing "autocratically," it is hard to understand how he could have done otherwise, given that the constitutional court had reversed the results of the national assembly election and disbanded the legislature. By definition, a president who must govern without a legislature is an autocrat; and we now know that the constitutional court was acting in close collusion with the military.[18]

The opposition harshly criticized as "pharaonic" the November 22 presidential decree that nominally placed Morsi outside the control of the constitutional court and hence in some sense above the law.[19] Yet the decree was sharply time limited, written to expire as soon as the constitution was ratified. It was issued against the backdrop of the near certainty that the constitutional court was poised to disqualify the constitutional drafting body, as it had disqualified the first body constituted for the purpose as well as the national assembly. If that had occurred, the constitutional court would have been able to effectuate a legal coup d'état that would surely have brought down Morsi. Thus, both the decree and the rushed constitutional drafting process could be construed as defensive attempts to preserve Morsi's presidency as well as the democratic will of the people who elected him. Both also protected the members of the national assembly, who then ratified the constitutional draft that the Brotherhood-dominated drafting body produced.

Given that Morsi was a legitimate, democratically elected president, it would seem on the surface that the attempts to remove him by public protests, even if they recalled the first Tahrir movement, could not be considered manifestations of the Egyptian popular will as a normative matter. What is more, it seems likely that many of the people who identified with the June 30 movement were different people from those who identified with the January 25 movement that had called for the overthrow of Mubarak. Of course, there was some overlap: it is possible to identify a number of high-profile "liberal" activists who participated in both movements and blogged and posted about it. Yet there is also credible evidence that many June 30 supporters and protesters were former Mubarak regime supporters who wanted a return to the pre-Morsi political order.

Seen through the lens of Morsi's democratic legitimacy and the presence of old-regime supporters among June 30 adherents, a distinct and familiar narrative can be drawn from the events I call "Tahrir II": a narrative of post-revolutionary revanche. According to this narrative, revolutions like the one precipitated by the Arab spring are frequently and indeed almost universally followed by coordinated efforts to reverse their effects. Mubarak's fall was followed by democratic elections. Supporters of the ancien régime did not like the results of those elections. Acting in loose coordination with holdover regime components like the constitutional court and (some) members/leaders of the army, the supporters of the old regime fought back. They used the new round of Tahrir protests to delegitimize the democratically elected government, after which the military undertook a new, second coup—and this time imposed its own government.

The relevant and salient fact about the revanchist narrative is that it sounds as though it must be patently illegitimate from a normative standpoint. Antidemocratic elements of the former regime—*feloul* in Arabic slang—are not "the people." If the June 30 movement was intended to subvert democracy, it could not have represented a legitimate expression of the popular will.

Yet despite having held that view as the events were occurring, and despite my ongoing instinct to adopt this reading of Tahrir II, I want to suggest that it is too simple, and too dismissive of the popular currents of the June 30 movement. To be sure, those who were in Tahrir to oppose Morsi in late June and early July 2013 were not a representative sample of the Egyptian people. But neither were the protesters who were there in late January and early February 2011 to oppose Mubarak. In both cases, some self-selecting people presented themselves as speaking on behalf of the people as a whole. The question for us is, did they successfully and legitimately express the popular will?

I have argued that Tahrir I *did* legitimately express the political agency of the Egyptian people for regime change. Having advanced that argument, I find that I cannot avoid the conclusion that Tahrir II did the same. If the people willed the end of the Mubarak regime, the people also willed the end of the Morsi regime just two and a half years later.

I reach this painful conclusion by analyzing once again the two subparts of political agency, namely historical agency and popular legitimacy. The historical agency question is, this time, the simpler of the two.

By the summer of 2013, the army faced strong incentives to remove Morsi. Most important, in the aftermath of the ratification of the new constitution, Morsi's emergent government posed an existential challenge to the army's role as the sole popularly legitimate governing institution in the country. The ratification of the constitution would have led to new elections. If the Brotherhood won a plurality or a small majority in those elections, and formed a functioning, democratic government, Morsi would have had a credible opportunity to displace the military from its role as sole kingmaker. Put a little differently, Morsi and the Brotherhood seemed as though they had a credible chance of consolidating democratic power in Egypt.

The reason this threat to the army seemed real was that Morsi and the Brotherhood had somehow, against the odds, managed to use repeated democratic elections to survive the army's attempts to suppress them. Consider the chronology. On June 12, 2012, the constitutional court, acting at the behest of the army, had reversed the results of the December–January parliamentary elections.[20] Then, a few days later, on June 16–17, 2012, Morsi managed to win the presidential election, thus reinforcing the Brotherhood's democratic legitimacy.

Similarly, after the constitutional court's threat to the constituent assembly, Morsi's controversial declaration on November 22, and the rushed drafting process of the week that followed, the Egyptian public ratified the constitution by a vote of 63.8 to 36.2 percent on December 15 and 22, 2012. Turnout hovered at 33 percent, which was low for such an important vote. But once again, a popular election had substantiated the Brotherhood's claim to democratic legitimacy.

The upshot for the army was that Morsi needed to be removed—but through a process that would not cause the military to appear democratically illegitimate. The June 30 movement was the solution. Popular protests in Tahrir already had a pedigree of legitimacy as justifying the military in removing the president. The only possible goal for Tahrir II would be to repeat the events of Tahrir I. As the military understood—and as everyone in the square necessarily understood—the June 30 movement would provide popular legitimation for a new coup, this time to remove Morsi.

It follows that the people who went to Tahrir in late June and early July 2013 exercised historical agency, perhaps to a greater degree even than did the protesters of January and February 2011. The Tahrir II protesters knew that their actions would create the conditions for the military to remove Morsi from office—because that was the script that everyone was now following.

And without those protesters, the military knew that it could not remove Morsi, at least not without running the risk of appearing fundamentally illegitimate. With the protesters, the military knew the opposite was true: it could remove the president and say it was acting at the behest of the Egyptian people. It knew it because it had done so once before and been hailed as the people's agent for doing so.

And so, the people who took part in the Tahrir II movement were historical agents of Morsi's removal. Were they also the political agents of it? That is, were they "the people" in the same way as the Tahrir I protesters?

The answer, I think, is that they were—much as I would love to deny it. Their numbers were comparable; according to some reports they were much larger. Protests on June 30 took place across the country, not only in Cairo (as indeed did the Tahrir I protests). The counterprotests organized by the Muslim Brotherhood were far smaller. But the numbers are not the only element of the normative aspect. Normatively, the protesters' claim to speak on behalf of the people was valid *because it expressed a popular repudiation of the results of a series of formally democratic elections.* That desire stemmed not merely from former Mubarak regime supporters but also from many activist liberal, secularist Egyptians who had participated in the January 25 movement and had previously seen themselves as favoring democracy.

If this formulation sounds strange, it should. Those of us who live in democratic countries are accustomed to believing (or being told) that "the people" only speak in the name of democratic-constitutional values and institutions. But, of course, that is quite wrong, both logically and normatively. When the people gather in the streets to exercise their political agency, and succeed in displacing existing government institutions, they can choose any form of government they want. Similarly, the people can repudiate any form of government they do not want— including democracy itself. These statements are true as a descriptive matter. Normatively, they rest on the idea that the people exist before and outside of institutionalized democracy.

They may self-govern through agreed-on processes and norms. Or they may break those norms and choose others.

Make no mistake, that is what the June 30 movement achieved—and was meant to achieve. The people in the streets intended to send the message that the repeated democratic elections of the previous two years had produced results they did not like. They sought to communicate that they wanted the democratic process to be reversed. The proof is that the people left no doubt that the entity they were calling upon to reverse that process was the military. That made the movement very different from a protest calling for a president to resign voluntarily or be democratically recalled, or presenting a petition demanding redress. The universal understanding that people were calling for the military to remove Morsi turned the protests into a rejection of electoral democracy itself. Euphemisms aside, one cannot call for reversing the outcome of repeated democratic elections by military force and still profess an allegiance to electoral democracy. The whole point of electoral democracy is for election results to stand even when they are not the results one would have desired.

Therefore, I want to reject the idea, however appealing, that the Egyptian people could not have been speaking on June 30 because the people were opposing the results of normatively legitimate democratic elections. The fact that I, as a constitutional democrat, am normatively committed to the validity of the results of free and fair elections does not mean that everyone must agree with me. A theory of political agency cannot rest on the assumption that the people may only act when they act as I wish they would.

Simply put, I believe the Egyptian people who exercised political agency through the June 30 movement and Tahrir II got it wrong. I believe now, and believed and wrote at the time, that they were making a historic error of the greatest consequence by repudiating their own democratic process. But that was the choice that the Egyptian people made. It would be presumptuous and condescending to argue that the Egyptian people could not have made this choice because the choice was the wrong one. That is not how political agency works. To be meaningful, political agency must include genuine choice—including the choice to act wrongly.

Agency and Error

I recognize the claim that I am now advancing—that the Egyptian people exercised political agency to reject democracy in Tahrir II—is at least counterintuitive, and arguably antidemocratic. So let me address several counterarguments directly.

The first and simplest counterargument is that it is a mistake to view Tahrir II as a display of Egyptian popular will or collective political agency. The Morsi government had opponents, many of them supporters of the old Mubarak regime. They took advantage of Morsi's errors, forced and unforced, and went to the streets claiming to speak on behalf of the people. The army used the protests as an excuse to remove Morsi. The Egyptian people had nothing (or almost nothing) to do with it.

This objection, which I take extremely seriously, can be interpreted in one of two forms. The first version admits that Tahrir I was a genuine expression of Egyptian political agency, while insisting that Tahrir II was an illegitimate coup. The second version denies that *either* Tahrir I *or* Tahrir II can be plausibly construed to express the will of the Egyptian people. According to the second view, the Egyptian public was always deeply divided. First one side took to the streets, opening the door to the army; then the other side followed suit, with the same result.

The first version of this objection is highly appealing because it matches the normative impulse to treat the overthrow of the dictator as popular and the overthrow of a democratically elected president as the action of old-regime loyalists. But it founders on the basic problem of parallelism. In both Tahrir I and Tahrir II, people went into the square claiming to speak on behalf of the Egyptian people. In both instances, we can acknowledge, at least some Egyptians, and possibly many, were not completely on board with what the protesters were claiming. But through the combination of decisive political action and a credible claim that the people should have the right to shape their own political fate, the Egyptian people spoke in Tahrir I. When the time came for Tahrir II, the same conditions applied. The political action was decisive. So was the claim that the people wanted to shape their own fate—this time, by removing Morsi.

Here is why the two episodes cannot be differentiated simply by the fact that Morsi was democratically elected: because normatively speaking, the people have every bit as much right to overturn democratic elections—or democracy itself—as they do to choose democracy in the first place. The underlying theory of democracy—that the people have the right to self-determine—cannot be reduced to the narrow claim that the people have the right to vote in elections and then must wait until the next election to change their government. If the people had the right to rise against Mubarak, they had the right to rise against Morsi.

Another way to think of this point is to realize that democracy is more than just a set of electoral procedures or institutions. To be sure, once a democratic government is up and running and consolidated, that is how the system of democracy starts to function. It acquires rules, norms, practices, and even laws that specify how elections work and transitions occur. The field of legal-academic study called "election law" or more grandly "the law of democracy" tends to insist that these rules, which it analyzes and codifies, are necessary conditions of democracy itself.

But that is not correct, because when democracy self-presents as collective political agency in a moment of revolution, it is definitively *outside* the rules of any game.* As we shall see in more detail in the case of Tunisia, the successful creation of democracy out of autocracy is precisely a process of finding ways to act collectively when there are no rules or customs or familiar norms in place to guide the process. What makes successful democratic self-creation so extraordinary—and so extraordinarily difficult— is precisely that it requires collective action by competing parties who must shape a set of rules and norms that all can grudgingly accept, all without the benefit of a veil of ignorance to force them into "fairness."

The unsuccessful effort to create and consolidate democracy, as in Egypt, has the same feature of operating outside any agreed-upon rules. The people called for Mubarak's ouster without having any preset plan or shared blueprint for what would happen next. Holding elections and choosing a president was one option.

---

* Nor can the meaning of "democracy" convincingly be tweaked so that the term comes to mean something like "liberal egalitarian and constitutional democracy." According to this approach, best pursued by the late great Ronald Dworkin, democracy itself entails basic rights and commitments to equality and liberty. There is therefore no contradiction between respecting those demands and following laws enacted by elected representatives. This approach is highly attractive from a morally normative standpoint, since it forces us to ask why we would want to treat collective self-determination as more important than individual rights. Yet the Dworkinian approach does not yield much in the way of normative insight if applied to revolutionary moments like Tahrir I or II, except to say (perhaps) that no one making a revolution should violate individual liberty or equality. The legitimacy or illegitimacy of a revolutionary movement cannot be judged in terms of the rights being protected until *after* a new regime has been generated.

Going to the streets and calling for that president to be removed was another option. In the end, both options were exercised, one after the other.

In between, there occurred a popular ratification of a constitution. That is the formal procedure that law-of-democracy scholars tell us should set the rules of the game. In practice, the ratification of the Morsi constitution meant almost nothing. The document did not constitute an agreement to settle the rules of the game. The people were speaking in Tahrir I, and by the time Tahrir II came around, they were speaking still. *Because democracy was never consolidated, the revolutionary situation continued.* The people were exercising legitimate agency all along.

From the standpoint of democracy as self-determination, this second round was every bit as legitimate as the first—and indeed had to be. That is because a self-determining people that can bind itself by the creation of constitutional rules can also, by the same logic, unbind itself whenever it wants. A familiar metaphor compares a constitution to Odysseus binding himself to the mast of his ship so that he would be able to resist the song of the sirens. But this metaphor conveniently omits the reality that the people may be stronger than the bonds they set for themselves. When the people demand revolutionary change and break the bonds— or when, as in the case of the Morsi constitution, the bonds were weak and haphazardly tied in the first place—the people can legitimately set themselves free.

Seen from this perspective, Tahrir II embodied one of the deepest and oldest critiques of democracy: that the people are too fickle to rule themselves. Having overthrown Mubarak and elected Morsi, the people turned against institutional democracy itself. By overthrowing the democratically elected president, they ushered in the army, which was only too happy to take away the people's right to self-determination.

The only answer I can offer to this critique is that the abandonment of democracy in Tahrir II was itself a democratic act. Some in the crowd probably believed they were supporting democracy against the Brotherhood's usurpations. Others, more realistic about what was coming, may have judged that the Egyptian people were in need of the army because they could not be trusted to self-govern democratically. Tahrir II was not fickle, on this latter view. It reflected the considered judgment of the Egyptian people that a public that elected Morsi and could not consolidate democracy should not be governed by democratic means going forward. So the Egyptian popular choice to return to military rule did not reflect the mutability of the political will so much as its mature self-knowledge.

I do not know which is more upsetting: the idea that the Egyptian people made a disastrous error of overthrowing Morsi and guaranteeing a new dictatorship because they were naïve and fickle or the idea that the Egyptian people abandoned democracy because they did not think they were capable of sustaining it. But if you believe, as I do, that Tahrir I was a genuine exercise of political agency, then you must accept that Tahrir II was as well. And if you accept Tahrir II as an exercise of political agency, then I am afraid you must adopt one of these two readings of what the Egyptian people's decision meant.

By now you may want to avoid the horns of this dilemma by adopting the second version of the counterargument we have been considering: that there was no political agency in Tahrir *either* time. To adopt this approach, you might not have to abandon the notion of political agency altogether. You just have to maintain that, in deeply divided societies, the concept does not contribute meaningfully to analysis of the course of political events. Where there is no societal consensus, runs the argument, there can be no political agency.

The objection is undoubtedly a strong one. It certainly seems plausible to say that if only half of a political society wills some outcome, and the other half wills the opposite, neither can be viewed as the normatively genuine will of the people. Nor is it necessary for these numbers to be exact. Approximately half on each side seems sufficient to refute the applicability of the notion of popular will.

Note that this is different from a situation where half a political society wills something and the other half is inert or uncaring. On my account of political agency, no strict numerical threshold—including numerical majority—is required to specify the exercise of collective political will. If those who care to act determine outcomes and do so on behalf of the people, that is more than sufficient. The hard case is one in which two opposing sides of the people each claim to act as agents of the whole people.

In response to this counterargument, I would like to concede that in a truly divided society, neither side can correctly claim to speak on behalf of the whole. But I want to argue that, despite superficial appearances, Egypt during the period stretching from Tahrir I to Tahrir II was not such a divided society. Rather, a decisive collective "people" genuinely sought the overthrow of Mubarak, and a decisive collective "people" genuinely sought the overthrow of Morsi. Not all of the participants in each of the collectives were exactly the same. But many vocal activists were in fact the same people. And similar coalitions of liberal elites and ordinary middle-class Egyptians shaped the January 25 movement and the June 30 movement.

This claim is tricky, because it is in large part empirical—and there is at present no very exact way to measure or assess the demographics of the protesters in either phase. The claim, therefore, must necessarily be impressionistic, and susceptible to revision. Nevertheless, I think there is considerable circumstantial evidence showing that while Tahrir I and Tahrir II did not share identical composition, they overlapped enough to establish both as genuine expressions of popular will.

The first key to making sense of the relationship between the two waves of protest is to note the absence of political Islamists from the vanguard of either one. As has been noted by multiple scholars and observers, the Arab spring in Egypt was not the result of coordinated action by the Muslim Brotherhood or other groups advocating political Islam. Rather, while the early Tahrir I protests were building momentum, the leadership of the Brotherhood made a conscious tactical choice not to be visibly present in the square, notwithstanding the movement's hatred of Mubarak and eagerness for political change.

The Brotherhood leadership feared, reasonably, that their presence would enable the Mubarak regime to discredit the protests as Islamist and use this excuse to put down the protests violently. It also feared that the protests might not ultimately be successful in removing Mubarak. In that scenario, the Brotherhood did not wish to be suppressed by the regime after the fact for having openly sought the president's ouster. Ultimately, late in the trajectory of Tahrir I but before Mubarak was removed from office, the Brotherhood rethought its tactics in the light of events and entered the square visibly. Failing to do so would have weakened the Muslim Brotherhood considerably in the elections that, everyone hoped, would follow the removal of the regime.

The reason the Brotherhood's absence in the early Arab spring protests is so significant for our purposes is that the Brotherhood was subsequently absent from the Tahrir II protests. Indeed, the Tahrir II protests were to a large degree intended and understood to be protests against the Brotherhood itself, embodied in the

Morsi presidency. Had the Brotherhood played a major role in removing Mubarak, won subsequent popular votes, and then opposed the removal of Morsi, it would be nearly impossible to argue, as I am, that the Egyptian people collectively acted both times.

Yet the fact that the Brotherhood won a slim majority or plurality of votes multiple times *after* Tahrir I does not show that the Brotherhood was instrumental in the Arab spring—or even that the organization was capable of speaking on behalf of the Egyptian people after it won those votes. Rather, the Muslim Brotherhood was simply the political organization that the largest number of Egyptians favored in multiple elections *relative* to the other political organizations that advanced candidates. Winning an election, or even several, is very different from manifestly speaking on behalf of the people.

Another highly salient fact about the composition of the January 25 and June 30 movements was the presence in both of secular-oriented elite Egyptian liberals. This vanguard never represented any kind of numerical majority among Egyptians. Yet its loosely organized members were more effective than anyone else in giving a voice to the Tahrir protesters—both times. Even in the age of social media, it is an apparently unavoidable fact of political mobilization that some speakers come to crystallize and stand for the views of the less articulate masses. Those voices may be expressed over megaphones or in social media posts, but their presence is necessary to the whole undertaking of assigning meaning to collective political action.

And on close examination, it is difficult to avoid the conclusion that Egyptian liberal elites strongly supported the overthrow of Mubarak and then just as strongly supported the overthrow of Morsi. The editors of an extremely valuable volume devoted to the role of Egyptian liberals in the Arab spring period put it bluntly in their introductory essay titled "Egyptian Liberals, from Revolution to Counterrevolution."[21] The authors take the view that "the ouster of Morsi was a decidedly *popular* coup."[22] They explain that before the Arab spring, many Egyptian liberals defended the Brotherhood "as a legitimate political force," notwithstanding their objections to the Islamist political platform.[23] Nevertheless, they argue, after Morsi's election, the liberals "radically shifted gears in their hitherto firm commitment to democratic reform."[24]

Much, much more could be said about Egyptian liberals—and the volume I have just mentioned indeed considers their post–Arab spring trajectory from a variety of angles. The editors' conclusion is, roughly speaking, that the liberals ultimately abandoned their commitment to democracy by embracing Tahrir II. Indeed, the subtitle of their volume goes so far as to speak of Egypt's "illiberal intelligentsia."[25]

A more precise formulation would not call Egypt's liberals illiberal but would rather note that there is no necessary alliance between liberalism and constitutional democracy. Many of Egypt's liberals did indeed repudiate constitutional democracy by calling on the army to remove the democratically elected president. Some may have imagined naïvely that the army would allow genuinely free, new elections and the formation of a democratic government. But unless they imagined somehow that the Brotherhood would be allowed to campaign freely and participate, and would lose because it had become unpopular, they must have been expecting unfree elections in which Brotherhood candidates would be barred from participating.

Others may have fantasized that whatever regime replaced Morsi's would somehow respect liberal freedoms. That would have made them liberals but not constitutional democrats. To my mind, such an expectation would have been fantastical to the point of delusion. Given that the army was removing a democratically elected Islamist government, it followed ineluctably that any new government would eventually have to suppress freedom of religion, freedom of speech, and freedom of association—at a minimum. This would not have been liberalism in any recognizable form, an analysis fully realized under the Sisi government.

Yet for our purposes it is essential to note that liberal activists did invoke a form of radical democracy in Tahrir II—just not *constitutional* democracy. The liberals' argument was that the people, on whose behalf the protesters claimed to act, wanted Morsi out. That is, the basis for the claimed legitimacy of the coup that was being sought was just as popular as the coup that removed Mubarak. The argument was that the people could legitimately reverse the results of the democratic election that had chosen Morsi and the constitutional drafting and ratification process that brought Morsi's constitution into force.

This radical democratic claim to legitimacy was, in the real world, a guarantor of future autocracy. But according to the view I have been advancing, that was all right with the protesters—including the liberal activists among them. Faced with the choice of democratic elections that had given them Morsi or a return to autocracy, they chose the army. Some no doubt did so with the full understanding that constitutional democracy would now be over and no one's rights would be respected. Even those who may have hoped for a better result nevertheless understood full well that the rights of the Brotherhood and its members were not going to be treated with respect. And even those so naïve that they could honestly say they expected new elections and a democratic do-over were choosing to trust the army to make that happen, instead of waiting for ordinary constitutional democracy to take its course.

I do not wish to dispute or deny that Tahrir II and the June 30 movement benefited from the presence in the protests of former Mubarak supporters who saw an opportunity to bring back a version of the old regime. I want only to argue that these supporters could not have been the determinative force in Tahrir II. There likely were not enough of them, statistically speaking, to fill Tahrir and other protest locations around the country. More to the point, no one believed the Egyptian public would be positively swayed by an explicit call to return to Mubarak's way of doing business. The focus of Tahrir II was on Morsi's failures and on popular will for continuing revolutionary change.

What ultimately made Tahrir II into a legitimate manifestation of Egyptian popular will was precisely the widespread sense in the country that Morsi's weak, ineffectual government was not what the Tahrir I protesters had been seeking. The Arab spring had sought the overthrow of the regime without saying what was wanted in its place. Now the Tahrir II protesters were saying, "Not this." They, the Egyptian people, were rejecting the state of affairs that had come to pass in the aftermath of their revolution.

The reason why is itself fascinating. I have already hinted at my explanation: no one made the revolution on behalf of the Brotherhood, and yet the tremendous first-mover advantage that the Brotherhood enjoyed in organized elections brought it to power. There was therefore a fundamental mismatch between the mood of the initial revolution and the realities of what the first democratic elections brought. That mismatch was predictable, given that, wherever relatively free elections took place in the Arabic-speaking world from 1990 until 2011, Islamists enjoyed precisely the same first-mover advantage.

Yet the explanation for why the Egyptian people rejected the results of their own elections and sought Morsi's overthrow is much less important in historical terms than the basic fact that the Egyptian public rejected constitutional democracy—grandly, publicly, and in an exercise of democratic will. No similar public, popular repudiation of constitutional democracy in one dramatic moment has taken place anywhere else in the world since before World War II. To be sure, majorities of the public in Hungary, Poland, and Turkey have voted for parties and leaders whom they understood to be trending away from constitutional democracy. But those parties and leaders can claim to have come to power without the need for popular revolution. The Russian public has clearly rejected constitutional democracy in favor of the autocracy of Vladimir Putin. But that took place gradually, in stepwise fashion, and Putin acquired his power with the sort of gradualism familiar to leaders who bring their countries from quasi-democracy to quasi-autocracy.

Egypt was, and is, different. There the people spoke, clearly and repeatedly. They rejected autocracy. Then they welcomed it back.

The political meaning of this epochal decision remains to be fully understood, both for Egypt and for the trajectory of constitutional democracy worldwide. In any case, taken seriously, it means that Sisi's autocracy is different from almost any other autocracy in the world, including Mubarak's. It may be validly criticized on liberal grounds for violating individual human rights. But it stands, for the time being at least, as a legitimate expression of Egyptian popular will. The people wanted the army back. Now they have it.

Conclusion: Autonomy and Agency

Through its inquiry into the meaning and consequence of collective action in Tahrir I and II, this chapter has sought to deepen the opening chapter's foray into the question of autonomous politics. First I tried to show how the space for Egypt's Arab spring was enabled by the distinctive conditions of imperial over-stretch and pullback, an aspect of my larger argument about the meaning of the Arab spring. Egyptians could and did seek to change their government without focusing primarily on what the imperial reaction might be. Their autonomy was a condition for genuine politics.

Next I suggested that this autonomous political action issued in choice—repetitive, iterated choice, in fact. Here, the goal of my argument is less to assign blame than to advance the idea that the decisions of basically free political agents demand to be taken seriously. Who the agents are and whether they have acted freely are always contentious and contested determinations, and I imagine I will not have convinced all readers on either score. But what matters much more to my overall argument is that the reader sees the plausibility of treating Egyptians' choices as their own. If the consequences of those choices were (to me) bad ones, they were nonetheless choices that mattered and had moral weight.

This chapter also offered an account of how the political Islam associated with the Muslim Brotherhood failed in Egypt—not purely on its own ideological terms but through the undermin-ing of the Morsi government and its own missteps, including its lack of effective coalition building and its rushed Islamic demo-cratic constitution. After Tahrir II, the idea that Islamic democ-racy of the Brotherhood's preferred type would come to prevail in multiple Arabic-speaking countries simply seemed impossi-ble. Egypt was the demonstration case. The end of Egypt's democratic experiment was also, I think, the end of the experi-ment of Islamic democracy in the region—for the foreseeable future.

Finally, this chapter also raised the specter of deep ideologi-cal division within a single people, a potential threat to the imaginary or aspirational unity of the people associated with Arab nationalism. As I mentioned, one could imagine that there was not a single Egyptian people speaking but two different peoples speaking at different times. In the end I think the best interpretation of the political meaning of the two Tahrirs is that the Egyptian people spoke twice, saying different things each time. The problem of pervasive division within the nation—and the tragedy that can result—is the topic of the next chapter, on the disasters of war in Syria.

CHAPTER 3

SYRIA AND THE QUESTION
OF FAULT

From the standpoint of democracy, it is tragic for a people to exercise its political agency, only to guarantee it will not be able to do so again for at least a generation. Yet the tragedy of Egyptian democracy pales when compared to the enormity of the tragedy that has followed the Arab spring in Syria.

The aspiration of ordinary Syrians to freedom and self-government was no less noble than that of their brethren in Tunisia or Egypt. In Syria, however, the Arab spring led to a brutal and bloody civil war that has killed hundreds of thousands and displaced nearly half the country's population. The consequences of that civil war include not only a transnational refugee crisis with far-reaching political effects in Europe and in the United States but also the rise of the so-called Islamic State with its transmutation of political Islam into a systematic program of genocide, murder, and rape.

How this happened will be an important part of my argument. Nevertheless, my focus will once again be less on producing a first draft of history and more on the moral questions that this history raises. In particular, I want to address a central issue that has received too little attention in all the handwringing about the Syrian situation: Who is at fault? Who, in the final analysis, should bear the moral weight of the horrors we have seen, horrors with consequences that will be felt for decades to come?

Again, my answer can be stated sharply: the Syrian disaster is the product of Syrian political relations as they have existed for more than half a century. The British and French imperial powers who created the map of the modern Middle East helped set the stage, to be sure. But they are not ultimately at fault for the breakdown of Syria. Nor, I shall suggest, is the United States, despite its manifest blameworthiness for the failure of Iraq and its failed "middle-ground" policy in Syria, which likely extended and escalated the civil war.

The blame for the Syrian civil war derives, rather, from the fact that the 'Alawi-dominated Assad regime was a minority-based dictatorship that fundamentally disempowered much of the country's Sunni majority. The logic of minority dominance— even minority dominance with the support of some Sunnis— made compromise extremely difficult in the face of popular efforts to change the regime: any challenge to the Assad regime was understood, perhaps rightly, as an existential threat to Syria's 'Alawis. The Arab spring brought war to Syria because the regime and the protesters alike quickly entered a dynamic in which both sides rejected compromise in favor of a winner-take-all struggle for control of the state.

History and Denomination

In Tunisia, Egypt, and Libya, the Arab spring began among Sunnis—but that fact was almost purely accidental, simply a result of the fact that the overwhelming majority of the population of those countries was Sunni, as were the governing regimes.

The motivation for the first Arab spring protests did not come from denominational or religious sources. The exception that proves the rule is Bahrain. There, the nascent Arab spring protests were fueled mostly by Shiʻi Arabs, a majority in that country, who were (and still are) subordinated to a Sunni monarchy. Elsewhere, Sunni identity was generally not an important factor in the emergence of the Arab spring. It typically went unnoticed and unremarked.

In this respect, Syria was different—different from the start.* The backdrop for the Syrian version of the Arab spring was the fact that the senior ranks of the Assad regime are composed disproportionately of ʻAlawis. ʻAlawis (or ʻAlawites, or Nusayris; the terms are interchangeable) speak Arabic. They identify ethnically as Arabs and religiously as Muslims. But they comprise a non-Sunni religious denomination, or sect, that diverged from other forms of Shiʻism in the Middle Ages by virtue of its mystical veneration of the Shiʻi imams. The necessity of avoiding religious persecution combined with the denomination's esoteric theology to create a culture of inward-looking solidarity based on secrecy, mutual loyalty, and distrust of outsiders.[1]

The ʻAlawis' specific teachings are not essential for our purposes, except to note that they differ markedly from mainstream Iranian Shiʻism (sometimes called Twelver Shiʻism). The doctrinal uniqueness of ʻAlawism matters because it has shaped the sect's distinct communal-political identity. That identity, in turn, has powerfully affected Syrian political history over the

---

* Yemen is a complex case. The initial protests against ʻAli Abdullah Saleh quickly took on a tribal character, and in Yemen, tribe is interwoven with religious denomination. The civil war in Yemen eventually developed denominational features, with Zaydi (Shiʻi) Houthis backed by Iran fighting mostly Sunni Southern Yemeni tribes backed by Saudi Arabia. Nevertheless, the early Arab spring protests were not distinctly denominational.

course of the past seventy-five years—in two distinct phases, each almost diametrically opposed to the other.

The first effect of the distinct 'Alawi identity was to push members of the denomination to closely identify with Arab nationalism—specifically, with the second-wave version of that nationalism embodied in Syria by the Ba'th Party, founded in 1947. To understand the affinity between Ba'thist Arab nationalism and 'Alawism, it is useful to recognize that many noteworthy advocates of Arab nationalism in both the first and second waves were *not* Sunni Muslims. Some were Christians, like the influential Palestinian writer George Antonius (1891–1941) and the Syrian academic Constantin Zureyk (1909–2000); others were members of smaller Muslim sects, like the philologist Zaki al-Arsuzi (1899–1968), who was a Syrian 'Alawi.

For these non-Sunnis, the appeal of Arab nationalism was partly that it offered a national identity that would include rather than exclude them. A non-Muslim or non-Sunni Arab could be as much a part of the Arab nation as a Sunni. Arab identity was also potentially secular, not expressly based on religion. In that way, Arab nationalism implicitly delegitimized traditional Sunni attitudes that treated non-Sunnis as second-class subjects. What was more, Arab nationalism offered a picture of Middle Eastern history that identified the spread of Islam not as the defining event of regional history but simply as a means by which the Arabic language had spread.

Second-generation Arab nationalism generated the ideology and movement of Ba'thism, propounded initially by the Christian Syrian intellectual Michel Aflaq (1910–1989), the Sunni Syrian Salah al-din al-Bitar (1912–1980), and Arsuzi, the 'Alawi. The Ba'th Party (*ba'th* means regeneration) joined the appeal of a nondenominational pan-Arab identity to socialism and a cell-based political structure well suited to the circumstances of the newly formed Arab states. Ba'thism flourished among young military officers in Syria and Iraq, both of which had seen monarchs deposed and replaced by weak republican presidencies.

In Syria, 'Alawi officers gravitated especially to Ba'thism. Secrecy came naturally to them, as did an orientation to small, insulated groups of like-minded believers. The neo-nationalism of the Ba'th ideology promised them full citizenship on equal terms with Sunnis. After the Ba'thist coup d'état of 1963, Hafez al-Assad, an 'Alawi officer, became commander of the Syrian air force. He participated in the 1966 coup that displaced the Ba'th Party's founding intellectuals, and in 1970 he took power in a coup of his own. Subsequently, 'Alawis came to assume more and more significant roles in the Syrian regime, particularly in the military and intelligence services. Though there were always prominent Sunni Syrians in nominally political regime leadership positions, over time, the 'Alawi identity-marker crowded out Ba'thist ideological universalism. By the time of the second Assad regime, that of Hafez's son Bashar, Ba'th power in Syria had become 'Alawi power—despite the fact that 'Alawis made up only 15 percent of the population.*

In this first iteration of 'Alawi influence on Syrian history, the Ba'th Party structure enabled a small denominational minority to capture the state apparatus for itself. At the same time, Syria was allied with the broader Arab nationalist movement. The

---

* The different trajectory of the Ba'th Party in Iraq shows in what ways this was a contingent development and in what ways a reflection of Ba'thism itself. In Saddam's Iraq, Ba'th Party membership came to be closely associated with Sunni Arab identity—exactly the opposite association it had in Syria, where the party became a tool to repress Sunni Arabs. Yet at the same time, Iraqi Sunni Arabs were a numerical minority in Iraq relative to Shi'i Arabs and Kurds. In Iraq as in Syria, then, the Ba'th Party structure showed its usefulness as a tool for a loosely denominational power grab.

motif of Arab nationalism, adopted and eventually exploited by the 'Alawi minority, functioned as an ideological justification for the state that deflected attention from 'Alawi dominance. Arab nationalist geopolitics helped justify and legitimate Ba'th rule at home, and hence, by extension, 'Alawi rule. Similarly, a strongly statist version of socialism drew Cold War military and economic support from the Soviet Union, while distracting international and domestic focus from 'Alawi domination.

The collapse of the Soviet Union, however, led to a fundamental shift in Syrian geopolitical strategy. For most of Hafez al-Assad's career, Syria had benefited greatly from its role as a nominally socialist Soviet proxy in the region. Assad had inherited this role as a legacy of Arab nationalism, which under Nasser in Egypt had presented itself as open both to socialism and to provisional or occasional alignment with the Soviet Union in order to resist Western regional hegemony. When Anwar al-Sadat abandoned the Soviets and allied with the United States as part of the 1978 Camp David accords, Assad was left as the standard-bearer for pro-Soviet Arab nationalism. The Israeli invasion of Lebanon, initially aimed at the Palestine Liberation Organization, morphed over time into a proxy war between American-allied Israel and Soviet-allied Syria, much of it fought in the air above the Beqaa valley, along the Lebanese-Syrian border.

With Soviet arms and subsidies gone, Assad needed a new ally to help him balance the regional powers of Saudi Arabia and Israel and keep his regime alive. In 1990–91, the gap left by the Soviet collapse led Assad to participate in the U.S.-led coalition against Saddam Hussein and to enter peace negotiations with Israel under American encouragement. Over the 1990s, however, the Syrian-U.S. rapprochement gradually faded, and Syria's interests began to coincide more closely with those of a different ally: Iran.

Even under the Pahlavis, Iran had regarded Saudi Arabia as a regional rival; and it continued to do so for geopolitical and ideological reasons after the 1979 Islamic Revolution. The revolution had made Iran staunchly anti-Israel for ideological reasons. Iran's interests and the Assad regime's overlapped. The Iran-Syria alliance was cemented by the gradual emergence of Lebanese Hezbollah during Israel's occupation of southern Lebanon between 1985 and 2000. Hezbollah, a Shi'i militia social service organization, and political parties, came to be funded from Tehran. Because Iran and Lebanon do not share a border, however, and the Lebanese government opposed the arming of Hezbollah, the organization had to be supplied via Syria.

The U.S. invasion of Iraq in 2003 ended definitively any prospects of U.S.-Syrian cooperation and further solidified the Iran-Syria alliance. Now both countries, each sharing a border with Iraq, became frontier states in the conflict with the United States. The implicit but existential U.S. threat to the Islamic Republic now applied to Bashar al-Assad's regime as well.

As the Iran-Syria alliance deepened, the 'Alawi identity of the regime reemerged in a totally new way. Now, the Assads could be seen, rightly or wrongly, as counterweights to Sunni-Arab regional dominance—simply because they were not Sunni. Iran's alliances in the Middle East, from Hezbollah to Syria to (eventually) Yemen's Houthis (themselves Zaydi Muslims), came to be organized around opportunistic connections to other non-Sunnis. This was partly a counter to the Saudi strategy of influencing Sunni states. It was also a consequence of the Iraqi civil war, as that Sunni-Shi'i conflict led Sunni-Shi'i relations to deteriorate dramatically around the region and the globe.

The upshot for Syria was that the regime's 'Alawi character was now aligning it with non-Arab, Shi'i Iran—precisely the opposite of the old Arab nationalist geostrategy that had been the initial result of the 'Alawi regime capture in the 1960s. Both times, the regime's 'Alawi character had been a key factor in its geostrategic decision-making process—it just had different consequences before and after the collapse of the Soviet Union.

Sunni Spring?

When the Arab spring began in Syria, it sought to present itself as a popular, cross-denominational, anti-regime movement. But the Assad regime from the start depicted it instead as a Sunni Arab movement arrayed against 'Alawi power. After all, the majority of the populace was Sunni while the regime was 'Alawi dominated. To call for the overthrow of the regime in Syria was, the regime argued, in effect to call for the overthrow of the Assad regime with its 'Alawi base. The notion of empowering the Syrian people to choose their own leadership necessarily meant empowering the majority in the country—a majority that was Sunni. In support of the regime's interpretation of events was the reality that the Syrian Arab spring did not begin in the capital of Damascus, where the regime-controlled state institutions were located and where 'Alawis and Christians (a regime-allied minority) had a large presence. The Syrian Arab spring began in Sunni-majority areas, like Der'a and Homs to the south.

I cannot emphasize enough how crucial and determinative it was to events in Syria that the Arab spring there came to be based on a denominational-sectarian divide. Although this pathway was not predetermined or necessary—and was arguably the product of strategic decisions taken by the regime in the first instance—once it took hold, it was essentially irreversible. The effects of this divide ultimately ran both ways, shaping the behavior and expectations of regime loyalists and protesters alike. With great speed, the divide functioned to foreclose the possibilities of responsible compromise that alone could have saved Syria from devolving into civil war.

For the Arab spring protesters in Syria, unlike those in Egypt, for example, there was no moment of idealistic faith that the military would depose Bashar al-Assad peacefully. The officer corps was mostly composed of 'Alawis, whose interests corresponded with those of the regime. The rank and file included many Sunnis, but not in elite combat units, which had been founded and trained with the dangers of coups d'état always in mind.

Thus, in Syria, Arab spring protesters from the start feared a harsh and violent regime response—a fear that was confirmed on March 30, 2011, when Bashar gave a speech that indicated he would take a hard line against the protests rather than responding with reforms or concessions. The protesters had in mind the example of the Hama massacre of 1982, when 20,000 to 40,000 people died after Hafez al-Assad put down a Muslim Brotherhood–led uprising using shelling, helicopter gunships, and tanks. This knowledge required Syrian Arab spring protesters to be especially brave—and to consider the use of force themselves, should they be attacked.

From the regime's perspective, the Sunni nature of the uprising meant that there was no obvious mechanism for a peaceful exit strategy that would protect the 'Alawi community from the potentially violent consequences of regime change. When a faction representing a small minority has been running a country for decades through a regime that relies on brutality to maintain itself, it becomes very frightening to picture what happens to that minority community when the government falls. At best, Syrian 'Alawis could imagine becoming a despised minority. At worst, they feared ethnic cleansing. Some hint of this possibility was captured in a slogan reported to have been chanted by Arab spring protesters in Syria in 2011: "Christians to Beirut, 'Alawis

to the grave." The chant may have been invented by regime supporters to frighten minorities into regime support, but in any
case it captured what minorities considered a credible threat.[2]

Could the Assad regime have sought a compromise, offering
modest internal reforms in exchange for the possibility of stay-
ing in power? According to one view, Bashar was uncertain of the
right course during March 2011 and seriously considered taking
a conciliatory approach before rejecting that option.[3] It is just
conceivable that such a compromise might have worked. Young
kings in Morocco and Jordan weathered the Arab spring by similar methods, relying on their monarchies' traditional skill at co-
optation and compromise. Attempting reform, however, would
have carried a major risk not only to Bashar but also to the regime as a whole, as well as to the norm of 'Alawi dominance.
Thus whatever Bashar might have thought the best strategy
for survival, he was constrained by the structural reality of how
his regime held power. When a former Syrian government of-
ficial suggested that Bashar could take the opportunity of the
Arab spring to purge hard-line elements in his regime, the president reportedly replied bluntly, "You are naïve."[4]

Was there a way for Arab spring protesters in Syria, for their
part, to signal to 'Alawis that the overthrow of the regime would
not lead to massacres or displacement? This is an important
question for determining whether the Syrian civil war could have
been avoided even after the Assad regime chose to describe
the protesters as Sunni jihadis backed by Sunni Gulf monarchies.
The answer is complicated. On the one hand, before the civil
war began, some protesters tried to communicate a message of
conciliation, inclusion, and peace. On the other hand, even if
those messages were taken seriously by their intended recipients,
'Alawis would still have reasonably feared that good intentions

would ultimately be overcome by animosity, and they responded by backing the regime anyway.

A parallel question is whether it is possible to imagine alternative 'Alawi leadership emerging that could have sought a compromise with the protesters by acting to remove Bashar, thus signaling that 'Alawis were a part of the Syrian people seeking change and should not be scapegoated in the aftermath of regime collapse. Again, some 'Alawis could have followed such a path; but they would have been running the risk that the Sunni majority would fail to respect their actions after the dust had settled.

The consequence was that the 'Alawi power structure seems to have concluded that even if Bashar were removed, they would have to substitute another 'Alawi strongman for him in order to preserve itself and the broader 'Alawi community. This in turn could not satisfy the Arab spring protesters, who wanted real regime change—not a superficial replacement of one 'Alawi dictator with another. Given a self-survival imperative, there was little reason for 'Alawis in power to break ranks with Bashar. Far better to back the regime in the hope of restoring the status quo that had prevailed in Syria for two generations.

It can be argued plausibly that Assad regime propaganda shaped the way both protesters and 'Alawis quickly came to perceive the clash between them as unavoidable.[5] Certainly the regime had every interest in spreading fear in order to pressure 'Alawis to remain loyal to it. And those 'Alawis who sided with the protesters were targeted quickly for retaliation by the regime.[6] Yet even without the intentional distortions by the regime, the logic of community affiliation during state collapse would have done much the same work. In Iraq, by comparison, after the collapse of Saddam Hussein's regime, Sunni-Shi'i communal tensions built to civil war even in the absence of any central power systematically seeking to create the gulf.

The upshot of this structural configuration of the Syrian Arab spring was that there was no scenario in which the military or intelligence services could or would remove the dictator-president. The Tunisia/Egypt model simply could not apply. Protesters either had to remain utterly blind to the consequences of their actions or had to imagine some other, alternative endgame—namely, the defeat of the Assad regime by a coalition of Sunni militias backed by regional powers, the United States, and the West. Regime supporters, in turn, had to imagine "winning" by surviving the civil war that ensued.

The Logic of Civil War

What made conditions even more ripe for a prolonged civil war in Syria was that both sides assessed—correctly—that they might win. Evidence that the Sunni protesters could have won comes from Libya, where Qaddafi overplayed his hand by threatening to hunt down and kill those who sought to challenge his regime. France and the United Kingdom, eager to establish a foothold as regional players while simultaneously asserting the doctrine of the "responsibility to protect" (R2P) under international law, led a push to remove Qaddafi through an air campaign. Barack Obama found himself going along, pressured externally by the political risk of appearing weaker than France and internally by R2P advocates like his U.N. ambassador (later national security advisor) Susan Rice and special advisor (later U.N. ambassador) Samantha Power.[7]

The fact that the Libyan uprising led Western powers to remove Qaddafi—even if it was only from the air—demonstrates that Syrian Sunnis were not delusional in thinking that the West might enable them to win by removing Bashar. Indeed, it was a highly contingent, uncertain process that led the United States, France, and Britain to decide against the kind of air campaign that they had launched in Libya. Even several years into the Syrian civil war, as Bashar's repression of the uprising became progressively more brutal, it remained possible that the United States would change its stance and remove him from power.

As for the regime itself, it judged—correctly, as it turned out—that the United States would hesitate to depose it by an air campaign. For one thing, Bashar estimated that Obama did not want to replicate George W. Bush's experiment in regime change in Iraq. The adage "You broke it, you bought it"—made famous by Bush's secretary of state Colin Powell as the "Pottery Barn rule"—meant that Obama would not want to author regime change in Syria, lest he own the mess that would follow. Similarly, Bashar guessed that Obama would want to avoid the possibly disastrous consequences of a destabilized Syria. Those could have included the capture of the Syrian state by an aggressive jihadi-Salafi regime and/or a genocide against Syrian 'Alawis and Christians.

The test of Obama's resolve came in August 2013, when Bashar used chemical weapons against Sunni civilians in a Damascus suburb.* Obama had labeled the use of chemical weapons a "red line" that Bashar must not cross—yet he did not significantly alter U.S. policy in Syria in the attack's aftermath. This was because the use of the weapons did not alter the underlying strategic logic of Obama's concerns about what would happen in a

---

* Whether Assad in fact used the weapons has become a highly politicized controversy. I rely here on the assessments of U.S. intelligence services (see White House report, August 30, 2013), as well as human rights organizations, recognizing that there can be no easy "objective answer."

post-Assad Syria—or about *who would be held responsible for what occurred.*

In the aftermath of the attack, Obama, under considerable political pressure to retaliate, instead chose to seek congressional approval for attacking Syria—approval he knew would not be forthcoming and that he did not try very hard to convince Congress to grant. This, to a degree, insulated Obama domestically from the criticism that he was abandoning Syrians to their fate. It gave him an excuse to avoid massive air attacks on Syria that would have had to bring down the regime or be viewed as having failed. Arguably, it also sent Bashar the message that he had gone too far, at least at that juncture. Further violation of the red line would force Obama's hand and push him to try to remove Bashar—not because it served U.S. regional interests but because the president of the United States could not afford to be put in the position of having his demands flouted or repeatedly ignored.*

Obama's statecraft had the effect of revealing to Bashar what the U.S. strategy on Syria was going to be. The Obama administration's policy was to call for Bashar "to go" and to provide support for the Sunni militias that arose almost as soon as the Arab spring turned violent—but to resist steps that would lead to the United States being held responsible for the fall of the regime if indeed that should occur. To put it bluntly, U.S. policy was to strengthen the forces threatening the regime enough to keep them in the fight, while refusing to take definitive steps that would make them win.

---

* Indeed, Assad held back on chemical weapons attacks for some time. Not until April 2017 did the regime return to chemical attacks—but by then Donald Trump was president and the situation on the ground had changed radically with the intervention of Russia.

From the standpoint of military strategy, this policy verged on the incoherent. The United States was providing "non-lethal" aid to the Sunni rebels in the form of arms and training—but not, for example, sophisticated shoulder-launched anti-aircraft missiles (MANPADS in military jargon) that would have enabled the rebels to take down some Syrian aircraft. Moreover, it was actively encouraging further support to those rebels from Turkey and Saudi Arabia, both U.S. allies (albeit discouraging the provision of MANPADS). Yet it withheld from the Sunni forces the air support that might lead to their victory, thus keeping Bashar's regime alive. The result, intentional or otherwise, was to prolong the civil war indefinitely, unless some other actor chose to change the balance of forces. Although a few voices claimed this strategy of prolonging the civil war was desirable,[8] most observers could see that the likely result would be further regional destabilization—the polar opposite of Obama's stated policy of restoring stability to the region in the aftermath of the Iraq war.

From the standpoint of domestic U.S. politics, however, the strategy had a clear logic. Obama could not afford to abandon the Syrian rebels to be massacred by Syrian troops, shelling, and chemical weapons. The criticism from neo-conservatives on the one hand and human rights activists on the other would be too severe, and he would be perceived as a weak and ineffective president. Yet Obama also could not afford to remove Bashar because of the risk of owning the fallout from it. The only remaining option was to keep the rebels fighting while ensuring that, if Bashar did fall, the aftermath could not be laid at Obama's feet.

Notice that the issue for Obama was not primarily the real-world consequences associated with Bashar's fall but rather the political question of who would be perceived to have caused it. Had Bashar fallen quickly, or had the Syrian Sunni rebels been organized enough to bring him down with relatively minimal U.S. assistance, Obama would not have sought to shore up or preserve the Assad regime. The United States would have welcomed the collapse of a regime that was allied with Iran and would have tried to help stabilize and support a successor Sunni regime.

What Obama felt he could not do was directly cause Bashar's collapse—*because that would mean he could be blamed for whatever followed*. In other words, U.S. policy toward Syria was structured by the problem of moral blame, played out on the domestic U.S. political stage. George W. Bush was to blame for the problems of Iraq because he had made a conscious choice to author regime change. Instructed by his predecessor's example, Obama would not be blamed for the problems of Syria.

Fault I

Did the American middle-ground policy "cause" the Syrian civil war? The answer matters fundamentally for a moral assessment of events in Syria and beyond. The long civil war led to hundreds of thousands of deaths and casualties, as well as millions of refugees. It fueled the sense of an immigration crisis in Europe that weakened the already faltering European Union. The Syrian civil war also created the conditions for the emergence of the Islamic State. That process, to which I shall return in the next chapter, had major global significance in the trajectory of political Islam and even Islam itself in the twenty-first century. If all these consequences could be laid at the feet of the United States and its failed Syria policy, it would suggest that empire—specifically, the U.S. empire in its distinctively chastened post-Iraq state—continues to determine events in the Middle East.

I want to argue now that while Obama's Syria policy contributed markedly to the long duration of the Syrian civil war, it did not cause it. The United States was not responsible for starting the Arab spring in Syria. It did not begin the civil war and could not have ended it without taking enormous risks that might have left Syrians worse off than they already were. The Obama policy was misguided and tragic. Certainly, it did not improve matters in Syria. Yet Obama should not be morally blamed for trying to protect Syrian Sunnis without committing to the removal of Bashar. Contribution is not causation—and the United States did not *cause* the horrors that ensued there. The United States was not morally at fault for the results of the civil war, including the emergence of the Islamic State.

To see why this is so, it is helpful to consider what, in retrospect, were the two alternative policies that the Obama administration could have adopted in Syria. One was regime change on the model of Iraq or, more realistically, Libya. A massive air campaign would likely have succeeded in removing Bashar.* That would have been morally attractive from the perspective of preventing massive Sunni deaths in the civil war. But it would also likely have killed many 'Alawis and other civilians. And its consequences on the ground would have been difficult to fully anticipate. Perhaps free Syrian forces could have produced an effective governing coalition on their own. But more likely not. No such result occurred in Iraq or Libya. A more plausible outcome would have been further fighting or an 'Alawi insurgency.

---

* A formal no-fly zone would have resembled the middle policy. Bashar's massacres did not come primarily from his air force (which was mostly grounded) but rather from shelling and ground troops. In areas where Syrian troops could not go, the civil war flourished between Islamic State, Jabhat al-Nusra, FSA, and Kurdish militias.

Certainly, the ethnic cleansing of 'Alawis and Christians was a possibility that could not be excluded.

The other available U.S. policy was to stand back and do nothing, signaling to Bashar that he could suppress the Arab spring protesters as violently as he wished. This approach would likely not have blocked a civil war, since Syrian Sunnis would still have risen against Bashar, neighboring states would still surely have helped them, and Bashar's retaliation would still have been violent. But strongly signaling that the United States would not help the rebels could arguably have saved lives by helping ensure that the civil war was brief. The Syrian Sunnis would not have been able to dream of regime change delivered from the air. When enough of them had died, the civil war would have ended in victory for Bashar. There would have been fewer casualties and far fewer refugees.

Some, or even many, readers may think that the United States should have adopted one of these two approaches to the Syrian civil war in order to have avoided prolonging it. But both options were also profoundly flawed. The former would have been morally appealing (to some at least) but massively high risk. The latter would have been deeply cynical but perhaps lifesaving over the long run. And it would have meant the abnegation of moral claims of any kind by the United States in the region.

Given these bad options, the Obama administration's choice of the highly problematic middle way should no longer look like it created moral responsibility for the events that followed—unless you believe that whatever the United States did, it would have been responsible for the Syrian civil war. To be sure, bombing would likely have caused Bashar to fall, with unknown consequences. Total lack of support from the United States might have hastened the defeat of the uprising, although regional actors like Saudi Arabia, Turkey, and Qatar would presumably still have supported their favored proxies. But declining to choose either of these forms of intervention does not make the United States into the prime mover in the war. One may have a moral duty to mitigate harm wherever it is safe and possible. But one cannot be morally at fault where there are only high-risk, bad options and one chooses not to take them.

In the final analysis, it was Syrians who rose up against the Assad regime. It was Bashar and his supporters who responded with violence and force. What fault there is for the civil war that followed rests with Syrians, not the United States.

That fault need not rest solely with today's Syrians. It would be wrong to blame Sunnis or others for seeking self-determination in Syria. It would, I think, also be too simple to blame ordinary 'Alawis for defending their regime and themselves against whatever would have followed from their defeat.

A better assessment of fault would look to the deep cause of the Syrian civil war: the structural reality of a denominational minority regime, governing for generations without sharing power. This structural reality, emphasized by a regime intent on self-preservation, made civil war highly likely once Syrians started demanding regime change with slogans like "Come on, leave, O Bashar!"[9] As I have argued, Syria came to be governed by the small 'Alawi denomination through the mechanism of Arab nationalism, specifically its second-generation, Ba'thist form. Whose fault was the historical process that issued in this arrangement of power?

Undoubtedly, empire contributed to the realities of Syrian politics. Like almost all empires, ancient and modern, the French in Syria played different ethnic and denominational groups against each other. 'Alawis were given responsibility in the Syrian military, creating a legacy that no doubt helped 'Alawis use the army as a power base in the course of the Ba'thist revolution and following it.

The Soviet Empire, in its turn, which sustained the Assad government for decades, also bears some fault for favoring the 'Alawi-dominated regime. The Soviets could not have cared less about the ethnicity or religion of who was ruling Syria, provided the government allied itself with them. But minority regimes are useful allies because they typically need external support to survive. This was demonstrated again after the fall of the Soviet Union, when the Assad regime gradually turned to Iran—which, although not an empire, also bears some fault for sustaining the Assad regime.

Strikingly absent from this list is the United States, which despite its brief period of engagement with Syria was never closely allied with the Assad regime and took almost no historical part at any point in shaping internal Syrian politics.* Syria is one of just a handful of regional actors that was never squarely in the pro-American camp in the past fifty years. That is not true of Iran or Iraq, and of course not of Saudi Arabia or Israel either.

The empires that did shape Syrian politics, however, also cannot be said to be ultimately at fault in the civil war. Although as a historical matter political structures linked to ethnic dominance have real-world effects, there are too many intervening events and actions initiated and accomplished by Syrians to make the root cause of the civil war—namely, the existence of the 'Alawi Assad

---

* The Central Intelligence Agency supported and arguably facilitated the March 1949 coup d'état led by military chief of staff Husni al-Za'im. But Za'im was dead by August. See, e.g., Hugh Wilford, *America's Great Game: The CIA's Secret Arabists and the Making of the Modern Middle East* (New York: Basic Books, 2013), 94 113.

regime—meaningfully the fault of the Ottomans, the French, or the Soviet Union. In the final analysis, the fault for the Syrian civil war lies with Syrians.[10]

Conclusion: The Age of Bashar

Nothing in the post–Arab spring fills me with greater terror and pity than the current (and likely final) act of the Syrian civil war. Victory for Bashar al-Assad is bad enough. But what makes it so much more pitiable is that this result almost seems like the lesser evil when compared with the alternatives. Vladimir Putin's air force has bombed and killed countless civilians. Some 5.6 million Syrians have little prospect of returning home from abroad. Another 6.6 million remain displaced within Syria's (resolidified) borders.[11] The areas controlled by U.S.-backed Kurdish militia are isolated, small, and not strategically sustainable over time. Yet the killing seems to be slowing and perhaps even coming to an end. This seems to be better than the available alternatives; and if that reality is not a tragedy, I do not know what is.

Seen from the standpoint of Arab or Syrian nationalism, Bashar's currently existing regime means something very different from what the regime meant before the Arab spring and the war. The "triumph" of Bashar is that he has stayed alive and sustained his regime for the 'Alawi community. Unlike Egypt, where the new dictator has more political legitimacy than the previous one, Bashar after the civil war has far less claim to popular support than he did at the start. Or, to be more precise, after killing so many Syrians, he has even less claim to be the legitimate ruler of Syria. Among the much-reduced population of Syrians who remain in the country, he might conceivably have a higher percentage of support than before the mass flight of refugees. But if this were true, it would only be as a result of a movement of populations unprecedented in the modern Middle East—the breaking of the Syrian nation.

The aftermath of the Syrian civil war thus demonstrates the hollowness of the nation that was supposed or presumed to exist before. Syrians, it turned out, could rather easily cease to act as Syrians but could begin to act as Sunnis, 'Alawis, Kurds, or jihadis. That is, the ideology of the nation-state could give way to alternative identities shaped by denomination, ethnicity, or religious orientation. The trigger was not precisely the same as the externally driven breakdown of security in Iraq after the U.S. invasion. Instead the trigger was the political action of uprising, coupled with the political action of violent regime repression.

This breakdown of the nation-state's ideology of identity could have occurred in other Arab states. Something analogous had already occurred in Iraq after the U.S. invasion, and decades before that in Lebanon in its civil war. A version focused more on tribal affiliation took place in Libya more or less simultaneously with the events in Syria. And Yemen's complex, ongoing civil war also reflects deep and multiple divisions in its society. Together the breakdowns following the Arab spring demonstrate the collapse of the very possibility of imagining Arab nation-states as stable entities reflecting common ethnicity, language, and religion. The reality may always have been the underlying diversity and potential for breakdown. But the passing of an ideologically shaped mythology is itself vastly important in terms of political meaning. Lebanon was once depicted as an outlier from other Arab nation-states, its civil war a reflection of a diverse population and geographic bad luck. In the era of the Arab winter, Lebanon looks more like an archetype.

With respect to this book's theme of Arab independence from empire, it is important to note that although the Syrian uprising was not against imperialism and was not directly fomented by empire, Bashar's survival was ultimately ensured by imperial means. Russia, the onetime imperial supporter of his father, Hafez al-Assad, had faded as a regional actor and become a second-class Syria supporter—but reappeared, deus ex machina, to save the son with direct intervention that would have been previously unthinkable. The United States, having mostly stood by while Syria burned, now silently allowed the Russian intervention—grudgingly in the case of Barack Obama, and then enthusiastically in the case of Donald Trump. An empire that is contemplating drawing back from its global role (as the United States is during the Trump administration) tolerates and sometimes even welcomes actors who intervene to end conflicts.

What is the most important political lesson of this bitter end to a tragedy of near epic proportions? For our purposes, the most important lesson is that a genuine will to legitimate self-determination can produce horrific outcomes. Even where the popular will seeks peaceful resolution, civil war and death can result.

One can try to place fault on the nation-state itself, insisting that a denominationally diverse polity like Syria was never viable and therefore could not survive the Sunni majority's attempt to self-determine. Or one could defer blame back to the imperially set borders that left the nation-state vulnerable to denominational competition and therefore drove collapse.

But both of these related narratives miss the point. Just about every nation-state on earth has had to overcome ethnic, linguistic, or denominational diversity in order to function. In most successful nation-states, some group has been suppressed, or worse. As for borders and populations, there is almost no instance in the world where the borders of nation-states neatly map onto population divisions, except for those cases where population movement or transfer was effected.

Nor does it make sense to harken back nostalgically to empire, whether Ottoman or otherwise, as a form of government suited to imbricated, diverse populations. The truth is that empires like to transfer populations as much as or more than nation-states do. The Ottomans did it in the fifteenth and sixteenth centuries, and again as part of the Armenian genocide. The Romans and Assyrians did it in the same region we now call the Middle East. The first Islamic empire superseded local cultures, languages, and religions throughout the region, not so much displacing diverse peoples as swallowing them whole and digesting many (though not all) of them as Arabic-speaking Muslims. There is no ideal past available as a model.

One possible lesson could be to embrace a cautious, chastened conservatism. Don't chance self-determination, the argument might run. However noble the aspiration to human self-determination, the costs are simply too high and the risk of incurring those costs too great.

Syria would then stand as an object lesson in not rocking the boat. Given that we do so badly when we do politics, maybe we should not do politics at all. Or if we inevitably must, let us do so with a strong preference for continuity and a high tolerance for injustice. Ultimately, this caution could lead us to reject the very ideal of political action as a defining goal for achieving human flourishing.

I do not want to neglect or deny the Burkean, conservative critique of political self-realization. The post–Arab spring tragedy makes it compelling. And the story of the Islamic State, to which I will now turn, underscores still further the risks associated with trying to make political change in an uncertain world.

CHAPTER 4

THE ISLAMIC STATE AS UTOPIA

If Syrians, not outsiders, are to blame for the Syrian civil war, the Islamic State poses a more subtle problem for making sense of causes and meaning. On the one hand, the Islamic State arose in the aftermath of a failure of American empire: its existence was historically connected to conditions created by U.S. imperial overstretch and failure in Iraq. Yet on the other hand, the Islamic State was the real-world, practical expression of a specific, modern theory of political Islam that was developed over decades.

The Islamic State's version of political Islam was, I shall argue, utopian, Salafi-jihadi, and revolutionary-reformist. It was also emphatically nondemocratic, very much unlike the Islamic democratic synthesis sought by the mainstream Islamists such as the Muslim Brotherhood in Egypt and Ennahda in Tunisia. The global and historical significance of the Islamic State thus derived, first, from the fact that, unlike Al Qaeda or other ideologically similar entities, it actually conquered and held territory and set up a functioning state. Second, the Islamic State put into practice a form of government that consciously rejected modern democratic and liberal norms as illegitimate and un-Islamic.

In its place, the Islamic State posited Islamic government as grounded in its own vision of the polity once ruled by the Prophet and the four "rightly guided" caliphs who succeeded him in the first several decades of Islam.

In this chapter, I begin by considering how American failures in Iraq set the stage for the Islamic State to be able to emerge as a sovereign, and hence as a caliphate. I then argue that the Islamic State was itself a manifestation of political agency by both the activists who founded it and the foreign supporters who flocked to join it. My argument depends on the claim that the best way to understand the Islamic State is to see it as a political theory—Islamist Salafi-jihadism—that found its expression in the form of a revolutionary-reformist utopian political community. This dystopic utopia had a brief yet meaningful opportunity to function as a state before international forces organized themselves sufficiently to destroy it.

The violence perpetrated by the Islamic State was thus undertaken by those who developed the ideology of the caliphate and then put it into practice. The Islamic State was not, I shall argue, a *legitimate* expression of popular politics or of the will of some identifiable "people." But it was nonetheless the self-conscious, intentional product of an organized group of people trying to give effect to specific political ideas and to govern on their basis. In this sense, the phenomenon of the Islamic State belongs to the tragedy of the Arab spring. Perhaps the strangest and most mystifying outgrowth of the Arab spring, it will be studied for generations to come by students and scholars of Islam, politics, violence, and the relationship among the three, long after Egypt's failed democratic experiment has been forgotten as a blip and the Syrian civil war has been classified as a denominational struggle of a familiar type.

Breaking Iraq

The Islamic State was in many ways an Iraqi organization. It was headed by an Iraqi who chose a nom de guerre associating himself with Baghdad. And for its military efforts and a good deal of its bureaucracy, the Islamic State relied on many former Iraqi Ba'thists in both senior and midlevel posts. Any account of its rise and significance must therefore begin with events in Iraq from 2003 onward and the role of the United States in them.

Let me state clearly at the outset that I believe the United States bears direct moral responsibility for the disasters that have taken place in Iraq, up to and including the emergence in the late 2000s of Al Qaeda in Mesopotamia, the organization that evolved first into the Islamic State of Iraq and then into the Islamic State. Indeed, American responsibility for instability in Iraq began even before the invasion of 2003. In the 1980s, the United States had actively supported Saddam during the Iran-Iraq War. After Saddam's invasion of Kuwait in 1990, however, which Saddam seems to have believed the United States would tolerate, the defeat of his armies by American forces in 1991 created conditions in which American responsibility grew further. The George H. W. Bush administration encouraged Iraqi Shi'is and Kurds to rise up in order to threaten and weaken Saddam—only to allow them to be slaughtered, after it became clear that U.S. strategic interests would be better served by leaving Saddam in power. Guilt over this act of abandonment, coupled with a desire to keep Saddam contained, led to the establishment of the no-fly zone, which in turn created a de facto autonomous Iraqi Kurdistan. Then came the U.N. sanctions against Iraq, championed by the United States and enforced aggressively by Bill Clinton's administration.

The cumulative effect of these actions was that, from 1991 through the U.S. invasion in 2003, the United States was acting as a (largely unfettered) imperial power with regard to Iraq, shaping its political geography and economy almost at will. That imperial stance was given full expression by George W. Bush's announcement that the United States could make war on Iraq "at a time of our choosing." The actual invasion of Iraq represented the apex of imperial disposition: dissatisfied with Saddam, its sometime vassal, the United States decided to overthrow him. Admittedly, the United States was a highly ineffective imperial power when it came to figuring out what sort of government it wanted in place of the one it had removed. But the incompetence and imperial overstretch that fueled the Iraq disaster were fully the fault of the United States.

The United States was also responsible morally for the sectarian civil war in Iraq. It broke out—as I argued at the time[1] and still believe—because the U.S. invasion and failed occupation created a classic security dilemma. By destroying the Iraqi state but not replacing it with any effective entity capable of enforcing order, the United States compelled ordinary Iraqis to find affiliations with groups that would protect them from harm. As it turned out, ethnic and denominational identities were the closest ones to hand for Iraqis, as they had been in the Balkans after the collapse of Yugoslavia. The sectarian divisions that became the basis for civil war did not emerge because they were "ancient hatreds" driving present animus. Rather, they were the most salient features of affiliation that made people believe there was a credible chance that they could be protected by their fellows. There was no lack of organizational entrepreneurs to convince people that this was so.[2]

More directly relevant to our question, the United States was also to blame for the ongoing instability of the Iraqi state, even after the troop "surge" that helped put down the Sunni insurgency by 2008. From 2008 until the fall of Mosul in June 2014, Iraq operated under a very fragile pseudo-consensus. The government in Baghdad, dominated by an ongoing Shi'i-Kurdish coalition, had promised local control and authority to Sunni tribal leaders as part of the grand bargain that helped end the Sunni insurgency. But the government largely reneged on that promise, which in turn rendered the predominantly Sunni areas of Iraq restive and dissatisfied. In truth, Baghdad's authority barely extended to the Sunni areas that had once been the hotbeds of the Sunni uprising.

True, the United States urged Baghdad to honor its promises to the Sunnis. Those appeals meant little, however, for the simple reason that, post-surge, the United States no longer had real leverage: the insurgency seemed to have been tamed, and the Obama administration had announced its intention to withdraw U.S. troops from Iraq. Republicans, who wanted to maintain the fiction that the Bush administration had finished what it started in Iraq, had little reason to complain of this withdrawal, although some warned it was too soon. The upshot is that no U.S. constituency was prepared to stop the Baghdad government from treating Iraqi Sunnis as dupes who had put down their arms and would now have to accept Shi'i-Kurdish hegemony.

The move by the Islamic State in Iraq to take territory shattered the illusion that Baghdad enjoyed real sovereignty, post-surge, over Sunni areas. Seen in this way, the rise of the Islamic State could be laid at the American door. If the United States was to blame for Iraqi instability, and if the Islamic State was initially an Iraqi operation, then surely the Islamic State was the Americans' fault. Indeed, Donald Trump's mad-sounding assertion that Barack Obama founded the Islamic State could perhaps be reread charitably to mean that Obama's ineffective Iraq strategy opened the door for ISIS to expand.

Despite acknowledging this possible interpretation, however, I want to argue that the instability in Iraq, which helped the Islamic State to break out and begin taking physical territory, cannot on its own explain how the Islamic State came to power. The majority-Sunni areas of Iraq had been unstable for the entire period from 2008 until 2014, and protests against the Baghdad government had occurred in 2012 and 2013. Yet during that period, the precursor to the Islamic State nevertheless lacked anything like the capacity to establish control in those areas and was indeed mocked by its opponents and competitors as a "paper state."[3] The distinct and decisive factor that led the Islamic State to its sudden new strategic position in 2014 was not the situation in Iraq but the situation in Syria.

What changed in 2014 was the possibility of creating a would-be state that bridged the Iraq-Syria border. That option emerged because of the continuing breakdown of the Assad regime's sovereignty over Syrian territory. That collapse was in turn a result of the Syrian civil war.

The story is complex but can be summed up simply.[4] After the death of Abu Musab al-Zarqawi and the collapse of the Sunni insurgency in Iraq, Al Qaeda in Mesopotamia had entered a period of hibernation. The Syrian civil war motivated the organization, now under the control of Abu Bakr al-Baghdadi and renamed "the Islamic State in Iraq" (ISI), to send a force into Syria that would build alliances and recruit local fighters. That force was named Jabhat al-Nusra, "the front for assistance," to signal to Syrians that it was there to help their struggle, not to expand ISI's territorial realm, which was in any case almost nonexistent.

On the ground in Syria, Jabhat al-Nusra took advantage of the near-anarchy produced by the civil war, allied itself with other

Sunni rebel groups, and began to conquer territory. As the group's success mounted, Baghdadi announced, in April 2013, that Jabhat al-Nusra was under ISI control and that together they would now be known as the Islamic State in Iraq and the Levant (*al-Sham*)—hence ISIL or ISIS, and in Arabic, Da'esh (for *al-dawla al-islamiyya fi 'l-'iraq wa-l-sham*). Although part of Jabhat al-Nusra resisted Baghdadi's claim of ownership and, in a defensive move, identified itself with Al Qaeda, other members of the group accepted the formal (re-)merger into the shape of ISIS.

By January 2014, ISIS had gained control over the Syrian city of Raqqa. Over the next several months, ISIS managed to take much more territory in northern Syria. Once its control there had consolidated, ISIS sent its fighters back into Iraq, gaining sway over much of the Nineveh province. In early June 2014, ISIS took Mosul, putting itself on the global map in a serious way for the first time. On June 29, Baghdadi had himself proclaimed caliph. His new entity, now named the Islamic State, already held territory on both sides of the Iraq-Syria border.

The key element in this reading of events is that what made the Islamic State into a meaningful regional actor was its ability to take and hold territory on both sides of the Iraq-Syria border. The softness of the Syrian front was what gave it the room to become an actual state. Only after establishing that base in Syria could the Islamic State create the momentum it needed to take territory in Iraq. Thus, without the Syrian civil war, there would have been no Islamic State.

Ideology and Agency

Each part of my interpretation of the Islamic State requires some further analysis. Each suggests consequences for the meaning of the Islamic State phenomenon, including its acts of murder and rape. Let me begin with the first: the possibly controversial suggestion that the Islamic State was an *Islamist* organization, in the sense that it followed the blueprint of a particular Islamic political theory.

Islamists, broadly speaking, can be defined as people who adhere to the slogan "Islam is the solution."[5] The slogan suggests that "Islam"—taken as a set of normative teachings, laws, and beliefs—can provide concrete answers to all pressing questions of contemporary life, in every domain. Islamists typically believe that Islam can solve the problem of politics, providing not only ideals and values but also institutional frameworks to organize even a modern political state. To be an Islamist, under this definition, is to embrace some version of political Islam.

The content of political Islam can vary extremely widely. The Tunisian intellectual and politician Rached el-Ghannouchi, whom I will discuss in the next chapter, has long considered himself a liberal democratic Islamist.[6] He rejects religious coercion and holds that Islamic politics should be deployed in a society organized according to liberal democratic constitutional values. He aims to "Islamize" society by the voluntary choices of individual believers acting collectively in social and political space.

The Egyptian Muslim Brotherhood offered a different version of political Islam. Although prepared to accept democracy and constitutionalism, it posited that the constitution should recognize God's ultimate sovereignty, require laws to reflect Islamic values, and prohibit laws that contradict Islam. The Brotherhood's short-lived Egyptian constitution reflected these commitments, which I have elsewhere called the democratization and constitutionalization of the shari'a.[7]

The political Islam of the Islamic State was something else again. It rejected democracy outright, rather than attempting to interpret or co-opt it. Instead, the ideologues of the Islamic State believed that they could build a functioning state on the model of the polity created by the Prophet Muhammad and his companions in the first several generations of Muslims—*al-salaf al-salih*, as they are known in Arabic. The commitment to the model of the *salaf* is the definition of Salafism, and it is what made the ideologues *Salafis*. The fact that they believed such a polity would be committed to fighting a constant war against non-believers is what made the Islamic State ideologues *jihadis*. Taken together, these features made the Islamic State *Salafi-jihadi*.[8]

It is not a given among scholars of contemporary Islamic politics to use the term "Islamist" to describe Salafi-jihadis of the sort who imagined and created the Islamic State. The reason is that the term "Islamist" has often been used to refer to Islamic activists who participate in mainstream politics, often by running for office. Until relatively recently, most Salafis rejected such electoral participation based on the theory that the Prophet's polity was not a democracy and their skepticism of organized political involvement.* What is more, contemporary jihadis typically reject any participation in political systems they deem illegitimate, believing that violent resistance is the only proper response to such a system.

Nevertheless, the Salafi-jihadis of the Islamic State were Islamist in the sense that they sought to create a functioning contemporary polity on an Islamic model. For them, Islam was indeed the solution, even if they might have viewed that particular slogan as discredited by its association with the Muslim Brotherhood and its democratic experiment. The Islamic State

---

* That has been changing since the post–Arab spring Egyptian elections, in which the self-described Salafi party, Hizb al-Nour, ran for office—fudging the question of how to be democratic and Salafi simultaneously.

was offering its own model of government as authentically Islamic and claimed validity for precisely that reason.

Thus the Islamic State was crucially engaged in a competitive dialogue with other Islamists, not least the Muslim Brotherhood, whose electoral victories in Tunisia and Egypt shortly preceded the rise of the Islamic State. The Islamic State was telling Muslims globally that its version of political Islam was the correct one. Like the Muslim Brotherhood, it was staking its future on the gamble that its polity would both govern and survive. And it was holding out its vision as normatively desirable (and, moreover, compulsory) for all polities of Muslims, everywhere.

This rhetorical and political stance of experimental Islamist idealism distinguished the Islamic State from the form of Islamic government that existed (and still exists, albeit under intense top-down pressures) in Saudi Arabia. The Kingdom of Saudi Arabia is definitely Islamic. The shari'a governs certain areas of law, and the Islamic scholars ('ulama') still play an important role in interpreting the law and shaping society. Yet Saudi Arabia's politics typically are not classified by analysts as "Islamist"—mostly because until relatively recently, scholars have tended to see the Saudi system the way it long presented itself, namely as grounded in Saudi and Islamic traditional governance rather than in the ideological project of crafting a new Islamic politics.[9]

The Islamic State ideologues sought to ground *every* element of their polity in formal constitutional and legal theories drawn from classic Islamic sources. Saudi scholars, when properly motivated, can do the same. Yet the project of the Islamic State was different in that it sought to construct an authentically Islamic polity on a classical blueprint *from the ground up*. That is very different from post hoc drawing on classical sources to make sense of a state. That is the model of the Saudi state, which drew on premodern antecedents while gradually consolidating itself into an effective modern police state. The Islamic State, in contrast, was a purpose-built Islamic polity intended to solve the problem of politics once and for all—and hence it was Islamist in a way that is not true of Saudi Arabia.

That is also why the Islamic State was *utopian*. Its founders believed firmly that a state and society organized on its principles would produce the highest form of human flourishing. That the utopia was intended to recapture the divinely dictated ideal realized in the original caliphate does not make it any less utopian. In this utopianism, we can begin to glimpse the second key aspect of the Islamic State, namely the *way* its political theory issued in a particular, real-world political expression.

Utopian states can take various forms. The Islamic State's utopianism was revolutionary-reformist. It was revolutionary because its exponents sought a total reorganization of existing social and political relations, including those governing personhood, family, property, and government. The Bolshevik Revolution of 1917 offers the classic modern instance.[10] Fidel Castro's revolutionary Cuba, in its earliest days, can serve as a useful mid-twentieth-century example.

The Islamic State utopia was also reformist in the religious sense. Its exponents sought a return to a long-lost form of religious community governed in close communion with God, through the proximity of the Prophet and his model as imitated and sustained by his companions. Like John Calvin's Geneva or Thomas Müntzer's Munich, which attempted to imitate the earliest Christian community as they imagined it, the Islamic State with its caliph enacted a historical-religious ideal of purity and perfection. Its members similarly experienced themselves as participants in a cosmically significant reversion to a divine ideal—one that left little or no room for deviation or internal challenge.

The precedents for religiously inspired communal-utopian reformism are Islamic as well as Western. Repeatedly, over the course of Islamic history, reformist movements have come into existence preaching renewal—*tajdid*—of originary Islamic principles and practices. A hadith attributed to the Prophet predicts that every century, someone will renew the faith[11]—and many have in fact tried. Some reformers have been individual scholars acting alone. Others have been leaders of movements that seized political power and created utopian or quasi-utopian communities.

Some of these leaders have been called or called themselves *mahdi*, meaning "guided," a reference to a semi-messianic figure associated with the period before the day of judgment and resurrection. The mahdi tradition includes medieval examples, such as the North African Amazigh (Berber) leader Ibn Tumart (c. 1080–1130), who conquered Morocco and al-Andalus and founded the Almohad dynasty. It extends into the anti-imperial struggles of the late nineteenth-century Sudanese mahdi Muhammad Ahmad, who led an anti-British uprising and governed a nascent state from 1881 until his death in 1885. His mahdist state remained in existence, expanding itself through jihad, until suppressed by British imperial forces in 1898.

The Islamic State leadership did not openly claim the title of mahdi. But in 2014 the leadership council of the Islamic State did declare Ibrahim al-Badri, better known as Abu Bakr al-Baghdadi, to be caliph.[12] The caliphate had been extinct since it was abolished by Mustafa Kemal Ataturk's Turkey in 1924, and the Islamic State's claim to have revived it had reformist resonance at least as strong as an invocation of the mahdist tradition would have had. In Salafi terms, a caliphate modeled on the government of the Prophet and the first four "rightly guided" caliphs who followed him constitutes the very essence of perfect government.

The Utopian Script

I stress the cultural and ideological precedents for the utopian revolutionary-reformist character of the Islamic State for two reasons. First, seeing the Islamic State through this comparative lens—both Western and Islamic—sheds light on the decision-making processes that led the exponents of the state to take the shocking actions that they did. Second, the utopian framework helps explain why many young Muslims from around the world, men and women, came to join the Islamic State: not despite its enthusiasm and excesses but because of them.

We know that people experiencing the elevated sensations and collective certainties of a revolutionary-reformist vanguard can commit acts that would otherwise have seemed to them altogether unthinkable within the circumscribed boundaries of their earlier lives. Under the right conditions, acts ordinarily considered crimes against persons and property become not only justifiable but obligatory. The execution and even liquidation of whole classes of people according to divine or "scientific" laws is not unknown. It occurred in medieval Christian millenarian popular movements;[13] and it occurred on a previously unimaginable scale during and after the Bolshevik Revolution.[14]

The murder and rape of thousands of innocent civilians by the Islamic State because they were nonbelievers can be explained in these terms. Consider the Islamic State's attack on the Yazidi community of Mount Sinjar in August 2014. A recent analysis suggests that nearly 10,000 people were kidnapped or killed. Of these, 3,100 are estimated to have died, of whom perhaps half were executed by being shot, beheaded, or burned alive. Of the 6,800 estimated to have been kidnapped, many were enslaved, including sexual slavery for the women.[15]

From a classical Islamic legal perspective, these horrifying actions were based on legal precedent. The Islamic law of war as formulated in the Middle Ages allows for the killing of nonbelievers who are not "peoples of the book," as Jews and Christians are. Because the Islamic State's ideologues identified the Yazidis as polytheists, they could lawfully be targeted for death. As for Yazidi women, the same classical Islamic sources allow for the sexual enslavement of female polytheists defeated in war.[16] The Islamic State demonstrated its formal reliance on these juridical sources in a series of legal opinions that applied Islamic law-of-war principles to their situation.[17]

Yet notwithstanding the formal validity of the legal texts on which the Islamic State relied, the reality of Islamic forces' conduct throughout the long history of the region was altogether different from the law on the books. It is difficult (if perhaps not impossible) to find any well-attested historical examples of such mass killings of nonbelievers anywhere in Islamic history.[18] Sexual slavery as a consequence of war may have been practiced in earlier eras of Islamic history, but it had essentially vanished in the modern period.

Hence, while it is technically accurate to say that the Islamic State murdered and raped on the basis of classical Islamic law, the mere existence of the doctrines in Islamic law does not suffice to explain how the Islamic State could have acted in ways that no group of Muslims had in the modern era. For that, we need to invoke the context of utopian revolutionary reform. Something further enabled and motivated Islamic State fighters to engage in extreme and horrifying acts, on a scale they had certainly never seen or perpetrated before. The added element was the distinctive, elevated mood and state of mind associated with the creation of a utopian revolutionary-reformist polity.

The murder of Sunni Muslims, simply because they opposed or were supposed to oppose the Islamic State, can also be explained as an instance of revolutionary-reformist behavior. Here, classical Islamic law provided no authorization or sanction for the Islamic State. The only justification seems to have been raison d'état, or rather the reason of the utopian state-in-the-making. Revolutionaries have long favored the adage that one cannot make an omelet without breaking some eggs—incidentally, a French expression traced back to the 1740s. It embodies the notion that the transcendent utopian ideal cannot be realized without a cost in human lives—and depicts that cost as inevitable, justified, and legitimate. Again, the psychological state necessary to engage in horrific acts is characteristic of utopian revolutionary reform.

Not only are revolutionary reformists willing and unafraid to commit extreme acts that they know would be condemned by anyone not invested in the same mind-set. They often seek out precisely such spectacular actions—spectacular in the sense of producing a global spectacle. Utopian revolutionary reformists want not only to create their idealized polity but also to be *seen* doing so. The world's condemnation, which they actively seek, is evidence of the world's attention, which is in turn evidence to them of the global importance of their project.

Utopians want the world to know what they are doing for various interrelated reasons. Most fundamentally, they want their actions to resonate on a global scale because they understand their undertaking as itself of global scale and ambition. They are, after all, creating a polity that is sanctioned by God (or by another comparably powerful authority) as the very model for proper human relations.

The Islamic State's destruction of ancient monuments like those at Palmyra fits neatly into this spectacular paradigm. A

Saudi Wahhabi-influenced strand of Salafism does call for the destruction of pagan worship sites as well as graves (including Muslim graves) that might be used as pilgrimage sites by Muslim believers. But nothing in classical Islamic law demands pulling down ancient structures per se—which is one reason why the antiquities at Palmyra still stood, despite more than a millennium and a half of Islamic rule. The Islamic State was trying to get the world's attention by destroying a globally known cultural site. It worked.[19]

For millennial utopians, who imagine themselves on the brink of the end of days, global attention is also intended to muster the armies of enemy opposition to the field. This millennialism was not, in my view, the dominant strand of the Islamic State's thought.[20] But it was present for at least some Islamic State thinkers, as attested by the importance that the movement symbolically attributed to the town of Dabiq, in Syria. The only religious significance of the town was a hadith predicting a battle between Christians and Muslims there before "the hour" would arrive—an association with Sunni millennial speculation about the onset of the end of days.[21]

Millennialism is an extremely common phenomenon among utopian revolutionary reformers. There are internal religious reasons for its common appearance, themselves related to specifically Judeo-Christian-Muslim traditions of apocalyptic thought. These traditions can continue to exist in secularized form, particularly among radical reformers coming out of (and purporting to reject) them.

Yet it is worth also noticing that one explanation for the recurrent presence of millennialism among utopian revolutionary reformists is that the rest of the world does in fact often want to destroy their movements. Utopian revolutionary reform by its very definition challenges the basic norms and values of existing human societies. That motivates many who are threatened by the challenge, locally and sometimes beyond, to seek the elimination of the new polity that is being created. In turn, the anticipation of this opposition can drive utopian revolutionary reformists into millennial mode. Having drawn the world's horrified attention, the Islamic State inevitably brought on an international plan to destroy it. And that alone may provide sufficient explanation for the millennial impulse that sometimes surfaced in the Islamic State's rhetoric, as in the emphasis on Dabiq.

Global Appeal

The utopian aspect of the Islamic State is also necessary to help explain why so many Muslims came from near and far to join the Islamic State. The number and demographic range of the Islamic State's foreign volunteers greatly exceeded those of the fighters who previously joined Al Qaeda or other jihadi groups to fight in Afghanistan, Bosnia, Chechnya, or Iraq. The Central Intelligence Agency estimated that there were as many as 33,000 foreign fighters who had joined the Islamic State in 2015, the height of the flow.[22] They came from Arabic-speaking countries, from majority-Muslim parts of Russia, and from all over Europe, the United Kingdom, and the United States.

The reason for the significant disparity between volunteers for Al Qaeda and the Islamic State is that their motivations were different—and the purpose of the entity they sought to join was different, too. Although the literature on volunteers for Al Qaeda is diverse and discordant, it is fair to say that earlier foreign jihadis joined Al Qaeda and its analogues to participate in what they saw as a global struggle against Christian, Jewish, and/or Shi'i occupation and domination.[23] In doing so, they also fulfilled an

Islamic legal duty of assisting other Muslims who were under attack by non-Muslims. Their actions, simultaneously religious and political, were focused on what they perceived to be *collective Muslim self-defense.*

In contrast, the young people who flocked to join the Islamic State did not see themselves as primarily focused on Muslim self-defense. They came with an affirmative rather than a defensive motivation.[24] Their goal was to participate in the creation of an Islamic utopia that would change them and the world.

The distinction between defense and utopian aspiration cannot be overstated. Jihadis who joined Al Qaeda may have hoped in a vague way to create a global caliphate in some unspecified future. But in real time, they were signing up to fight in a war or wars that could not realistically be won. They therefore had to assume an attitude of inevitable self-sacrifice. That is, they had to be willing to die for a cause whose victory they would likely not experience and in defense of abstractions whose concrete manifestation they would almost certainly never see.

There are, of course, people who are prepared to sacrifice and die purely for their beliefs and ideals. But the rootlessness, hopelessness, and alienation that characterized many Al Qaeda jihadis were important factors in contributing to this willingness. It takes a certain sort of character—combined with a certain set of bad circumstances—to fight in the name of God with little prospect of visible success.

Even where, as in American-occupied Iraq or Soviet-occupied Afghanistan, the resistance had some prospect of success in the form of defeating the occupier, a foreigner signing up for Al Qaeda–style jihad had to practice a certain kind of self-effacement. Others might benefit from the victory, but *he* would then leave, moving on to the next conflict. No doubt there is romance to be found in the ideal of the traveling warrior who fights the fights of others. But the true knight-errant can never go home, whether he is a jihadi or a Quixote. He fights for the homes of others. Psychologically speaking, he has no home himself, even if he might have a vague place of origin of the kind invoked by many jihadis in their noms de guerre.

Not so the foreigner who comes to join a utopian revolutionary-reformist community like the Islamic State. For him (or her), fighting and dying are not the point—the point is building. The true revolutionary reformist must be prepared to die for the cause, but his death is an unfortunate necessity, not an end in itself. The revolutionary reformist *may* become a martyr but does not necessarily *seek* to become a martyr. His first choice is to become a citizen or subject of the utopian polity that is being constructed.

Joining the Islamic State therefore did not require pessimism, hopelessness, or alienation, although those could have been present. Joining the Islamic State was an act of utopian optimism. To be sure, joining meant braving the risk of dying. The Islamic State was enmeshed in war and conflict throughout its entire existence. Yet from the first moment that it burst onto the international scene, with the conquering of Mosul, the Islamic State offered its volunteers the opportunity to live and act within an actually existing utopian polity.

To create and maintain this appeal, it was absolutely essential that the Islamic State actually held territory. It was not only that a true caliphate must have real-world sovereignty over some significant slab of physical space. The existence of a state-like entity, even if nascent and still developing, provided the premise for utopian living. Volunteers for the Islamic State were not going into the void. They were traveling into a place and time of unique, elevated polity construction—into the world of the Prophet and his companions.

A close modern analogy here is the idealistic young socialists and communists from around the world who came to join the Cuban Revolution after Castro came to power.* Their iconic model was Che Guevara, the child of the Argentinian bourgeoisie who joined the struggle even while Castro was still in the hills and emerged as a leader in the revolution. Other foreigners who followed later were motivated by the concrete knowledge that they would be observing and participating in the creation of an idealized, utopian Communist state.[25]

To observers horrified by the spectacular violence of the Islamic State, it may be difficult to imagine that anyone of optimistic character would want to join the entity that was perpetrating such acts. But one person's utopia is another's dystopia. To someone sympathetic to utopian revolutionary-reformist aims, violence may be attractive (or else forgivable) as a necessary step along the way to the creation of the new polity.

This analysis also explains, I believe, the presence of a non-trivial number of women volunteers in the Islamic State. Whereas Al Qaeda foreign fighters were exclusively male, imagining themselves as members of a holy warrior caste, it was perfectly comprehensible from within the framework of Salafism for women to participate in the construction of the Islamic State's utopian polity. Women were not joining the Islamic State to be warrior jihadis but to be active participants in state-making. No different from men, they sought to participate in idealized utopian revolutionary reform.

---

* One could add Europeans who joined the American Revolution for ideological reasons; foreigners who joined the French and Russian revolutions; or Americans who joined the Spanish civil war on the loyalist side. In several (though not all) of these cases, extreme ideological violence including spectacular executions followed the initial revolutionary impulse.

Again, outside observers might wonder how women could possibly be drawn to a social movement that openly embraced sexual violence and subjugation of women. But to those women prepared to join the Islamic State, the rape and sexual enslavement of Yazidi polytheists would have figured, if at all, as a seamless part of the Islamic State's utopian realization of the original Islamic polity of the Prophet and his companions.

As for the prospect of subordination of women in the Islamic State's particular version of idealized Islamic society, one can safely assume that women who volunteered to join the Islamic State did not view willful participation in a prophetic utopia as subservience. Rather, to live according to the shari'a in its purest form would be inherently liberating and divinely sanctioned. Even if the laws being applied to them on arrival might limit and constrain their choices, the women volunteers would already have engaged in an existential act of voluntary choice. They would have left their homes and families to throw in their lots with a community fulfilling the injunction to live in the path of God.[26]

Will and Power

Identifying the impulse and desire to make one's life meaningful by joining a utopian revolutionary-reformist community is not only a powerful explanatory tool for making sense of the Islamic State. It also can help show how the entire phenomenon of the Islamic State functioned as an expression of political will.

The claim I want to make may sound doubtful or even disturbing. Stated simply, it is this: the Islamic State, with its utopianism and its violence, expressed the political will of those who founded and joined it. The building of the state did not proceed accidentally or unintentionally but as the concrete

implementation of a blueprint well understood by the participants. As an effort of community-building and state-making,
the creation of the Islamic State reflected the desire of a self-
organized group of mostly Arabic-speaking people to exercise
agency and shape their own future in the sphere of politics.

In this crucial sense, the phenomenon of the Islamic State was
an inseparable part of the post–Arab spring moment, a moment
of variegated, multiple, and diverse attempts at political self-
expression by different groups of Arabic speakers—some
whole peoples, some smaller subgroups with aspirations to that
status. The creators of the Islamic State were attempting to act
as agents in politics every bit as much as the peaceful Arab spring
protesters or those who took up arms against oppressive regimes.
Indeed, the exponents of the Islamic State possessed what most
Arab spring protesters did not: a well-developed, specific vision
of the polity they hoped to create.[27]

Of course, in most ways, the Islamic State activists differed
from peaceful Arab spring protesters. Most obviously, they used
violent means and sought ends that were immoral and wrong.
But in other aspects, the comparison is illuminating, for commonalities as well as differences.

Take the question of *whose* will was being expressed. The will
to create the Islamic State was not the will of a preexisting nation. There was no *sha'b*, no people who could be said to want
to organize themselves into the Islamic State. There was no preexisting political boundary around the territory that the Islamic
State sought to rule. Indeed, part of the appeal of the Islamic State
was precisely that it crossed and in fact effaced existing borders,
most notably that separating Iraq and Syria, which the Islamic
State depicted, anachronistically to be sure, as a product of the
Sykes-Picot agreement.

Rather, the will behind the Islamic State was the will of a small, self-organized group of people who saw themselves as a vanguard capable of establishing a new order in the region and ultimately the world. That will unquestionably sought to establish self-government in a new political entity, connected to a new political community. The leaders of the Islamic State wanted first to incorporate Sunni Muslim Arabs in Iraq and Syria into a single community, and then to constitute this community as the kernel of a gradually growing, global Islamic polity.

The redefinition of ISIS into *the* Islamic State—unmodified by geography—expressed this second, greater goal. The declaration of a caliphate took the goal to its logical conclusion (even if its high aspirations ultimately failed). A caliphate is, by its definition, the sole legitimate Islamic polity, aspiring to incorporate all others into its political authority. The caliph claims legitimate authority over the entire Muslim *umma*, or community.

Unlike the national aspirations of the "people" of Egypt assembled in Tahrir Square, the Islamic State did not intend to include everyone living under its envisioned jurisdiction in the community. Non-Muslims would not belong to the *umma*. Polytheists, as we have seen, were to be killed or enslaved. Peoples of the book—in practice, only Christians—would be tolerated, subject to second-class status. This difference undoubtedly deserves moral condemnation. It is notable, however, that it represents a deviation only in degree from other nationalist accounts of self-determination, which also sometimes have involved ethnic cleansing, slavery (in the case of the United States), and the conferral of second-class status on some residents if they are noncitizens or members of an ethnic or religious minority.

Perhaps a greater difference from the more modest national self-determination aspirations of Arab spring protesters was that the Islamic State sought to transcend national boundaries to include all Muslims, and perhaps ultimately all humans. As I have previously noted, however, the "people" of the Arab spring slogan were also in some sense transnationally imagined. The "Arabs" are not the same as the Muslim *umma*: as a historical matter, the imagined Arab nation was a kind of substitute for the *umma* as defined under classical Islamic thought. It was both narrower, in its ethnic-linguistic restriction, and broader, in its incorporation of non-Muslim Arabs.

The point of these comparisons is to bring the story of the Islamic State into the broader narrative of the tragedy of the Arab winter. The story of the two Tahrirs manifests nobility followed by reversal and failure. In the case of the Islamic State, the political will to create utopian, post-imperial, transnational Muslim self-government would have been noble, too, if it had not been embedded in murder and sexual violence. Where the case of the Tahrir II reversal takes us from democracy to autocracy, the reversal in the case of the Islamic State takes us from self-determination (albeit horrific) to imperial suppression—and a return to the autocratic status quo ante of the Assad regime.

Conclusion: After the Islamic State as State

Ultimately, the combination of Western air power, Kurdish and Shi'i militias, and active Russian intervention from the air and ground in support of Bashar al-Assad brought the Islamic State to the end of its road as a territory-controlling power. From that point forward—sometime in late 2017—the Islamic State was forced to revert to the more familiar form of an international terrorist organization, essentially an updated version of Al Qaeda. Its global terrorist attacks aim to be comparably spectacular and comparably ubiquitous. They may well achieve that long-term goal. But those attacks no longer direct attention to the Islamic State qua state, since no such state exists. This marks a decisive change in the distinctive political meaning of the organization, which, I have argued, depended crucially on its actual achievement of statehood.

The Islamic State continues to exist through its offshoots that arose in other power vacuums, such as Afghanistan and Libya. But the groups bearing the name "Islamic State" there are no longer participating in the utopian moment, assuming they ever were. They borrowed the Islamic State brand, and now they are preserving it—for the moment—for their own purposes, much as regional Al Qaeda movements did after 2001. They would probably abandon the name when and if it ceased to give them a distinctive identity connected to the conquest and holding of territory.

That leaves the Islamic State going forward as something symbolically different: a powerful reminder of what happened when Salafi-jihadis took power and created a state. A movement that was made unique by being concrete is now abstract once more. A small number of Salafi-jihadis may look on the failed Islamic State with nostalgia and blame the rest of the world for destroying it. But even for such believers, it will be hard to keep up an idealized or positive depiction of the Islamic State over time. After all, God did not prosper the Islamic State, at least not after its initial rise. God left the state to founder and fail at the hands of its enemies. Ultimately, the Islamic State may be discredited by the very fact of its fall.

For most people, however, including most Muslims, the Islamic State will survive in memory as a dystopian failure. Its message will be that it was deeply misguided to attempt the re-creation of what the state's founders imagined as the original Islamic polity. Islamic democracy of the kind favored by the

Muslim Brotherhood failed in Egypt. The Salafi-jihadis' new-old state form failed with the failure of the Islamic State. Neither is likely to be tried again in the Arabic-speaking world, for at least a generation.

This development matters hugely for the theory and practice of political Islam. For nearly a quarter century, the Muslim Brotherhood and its associated movements and intellectuals struggled to formulate a theory of Islamic democracy. The Islamic State posed a Salafi-jihadi alternative to this ideology just after the Brotherhood failed in its brief run at governance in Egypt. And the political Islam of the Islamic State failed too, at least if viewed as the theory of a functioning state. In the time of the Arab winter, political Islam is now left without a noteworthy model of a state form that might actually work. As a set of ideologies, political Islam stands more discredited than at any time in the past century.

At the broadest level of political meaning, juxtaposing the failure of political Islam with the disaster of the Syrian civil war and the ongoing, unresolved civil wars in Libya and Yemen might well lead the reader to conclude that the Arab spring should never have happened. It is possible to imagine the view that the Arab world was unready for regime change in the direction of democracy or, really, any form of improved political life. It is even possible to drift from this pessimism into the still darker view that politics in the Arabic-speaking countries is permanently broken—and that this might have something to do with those countries' shared political culture, or with Islam.

I want to warn against the culturalist error of thinking that Arabs specifically or Muslims more broadly should avoid taking charge of their own political fates because they are somehow uniquely unsuited to success. The ratio of success in the aftermath of the Arab spring has been atrocious. Yet it has not been zero. There is one outlying case left to consider: the one where the Arab spring began. And the story of Tunisia has the capacity to make us revisit all our assumptions about how constitutional democracy and peaceful transition can occur in an Arabic-speaking country. Tunisia can make us ask: Why not?

CHAPTER 5

TUNISIA AND POLITICAL
RESPONSIBILITY

Imagine for a moment that the Arab spring, which began in Tunisia, had not spread from its place of origin. We would consider this "Tunisian spring" and its aftermath an impressive example of self-democratization by a people whose circumstances were not much different from those of many others in the postcolonial world. Contrasted with the failure of Egypt and the disaster of Syria, however, Tunisia looks like an extreme outlier in the broader, regional phenomenon that it started.

Tunisia's modern history begins as a city-state naval power, loosely associated with other similar North African powers known as the Barbary states. Like its neighbors, early modern Tunis was nominally under Ottoman sovereignty while in practice exercising substantial autonomy. Then, in 1881, France invaded and made the country a protectorate. Independence came in 1956 after decades of efforts repressed by France. Habib Bourguiba, a hero of the independence movement, ruled for the next thirty years as an autocrat presiding over a one-party, vaguely socialist state. In 1987 he was replaced by Zine al-Abidine Ben Ali in a bloodless transfer of power; Ben Ali modestly liberalized the economy while preserving presidential control over the state.[1]

This compressed account is intended to show just how superficially typical of the Arab world Tunisia was. Typical, that is, until late December 2010—when the frustrated fruit seller Mohamed Bouazizi self-immolated and subsequently died, igniting the protests that would lead Ben Ali to leave the country on January 14, 2011. The experience of empire and colonialism; the hopeful independence; the state-centered, semi-socialist economy; the slide into dictatorship implemented through secret police: these were all highly familiar elements of the story of postcolonial political life in the Arab world, in Africa more broadly, and beyond.

Tunisia was also typical in that what generated the protests initially was not a well-developed vision of political change but a more diffuse combination of social and economic dissatisfaction. Unemployment was near an all-time high of around 19 percent, a state of affairs particularly painful for an educated bourgeoisie accustomed to plentiful government jobs. WikiLeaks releases of U.S. State Department documents at the end of November 2010 revealed descriptions of government corruption and extravagant expenditure by regime cronies.[2] The regime's vulnerabilities were those of most postcolonial dictatorships stuck in the economic doldrums. On the one hand, there was no reason to expect Tunisia to break out into a significant form of revolutionary transformation. On the other, there was nothing particularly durable-seeming about the existing regime.

Given this context, what subsequently transpired in Tunisia is little short of extraordinary. In the aftermath of Ben Ali's rapid departure, secular and Islamist activists, civil society institutions, new politicians, and the public all engaged in a multiyear, slowly evolving, high-stakes process of negotiation and

compromise that led to the emergence of a relatively stable, functioning, constitutional liberal democracy. Throughout this process, numerous individual Tunisians as well as Tunisian associations, old and new, exercised political agency with a stunning
degree of responsibility.

One goal of this chapter is to offer an interpretation of why
that happened—especially when the examples of Egypt and
Syria make it so clear that a bad outcome was far more likely. My
approach takes into account a range of factors that have been
noted by observers worldwide. One of the most prominent is
Tunisia's relatively strong civil society, which was subsequently
implicitly credited by the Nobel Peace Prize committee for the
success of the Tunisian transition. Another is Tunisia's good fortune that the head of its leading Islamist party, Rached el-
Ghannouchi, happened to be an intellectual—one who had
found his way to political liberalism and who was able to guide
his party into a remarkable synthesis of Islam and democracy.
Tunisia also benefited from a political culture that came to be
informed and even obsessed by the idea of consensus, a political culture arguably more likely to be found in a small, mostly
homogeneous country with a relatively compact political elite.[3]

Yet the overarching interpretation that I shall advance goes
beyond institutions and individuals. It is, rather, an interpretation grounded in the moral theory of political action. I want to
argue that Tunisia succeeded because its citizens exercised not
only political agency but also political responsibility. That is,
Tunisians—protesters, activists, civil society leaders, politicians,
voters—did more than attempt to shape the course of their governance through their collective action. They realized that they
must take into account the probable consequences of each step
of their decision making. No one in Tunisia expected the world
to come to their aid, on any side of the political spectrum.

Tunisians also believed, correctly, that if their efforts failed they alone would bear the consequences. That moderated their aspirations and tempered their potential intransigence. Everyone had to compromise in order to avoid breakdown; so everyone did.

Mostly, then, the Tunisian story is one of modest, chastened heroism—the heroism of compromise, not the heroism of standing up for abstract principles. Yet alongside that heroic story run several countercurrents—each of which suggests the limits and challenges of what Tunisia has already accomplished.

One is the rise of Salafi-jihadism in a country that previously seemed to have comparatively little interest in, or manifestation of, the phenomenon. It has been widely reported that more Tunisians went to join the Islamic State than citizens of any other country—perhaps as many as six thousand.[4] There have also been several high-profile terrorist attacks within Tunisia itself. This noteworthy development reflects, I will suggest, both the costs of rapid liberalization and the special attraction of transformational utopianism in a place where change is in the air.

Another, more significant countercurrent has to do with the consequences of the Tunisian revolution. The protesters went to the streets seeking jobs and social justice, and believing that regime change would bring both. What they got was constitutional democracy with elected politicians. Yet liberal democracies do not have any magic solution for facilitating economic development in a country like Tunisia, which has a high cost of labor but lacks any particularly significant comparative advantage in production relative to its neighbors.

Thus there was (and still is) a type of mismatch between what Tunisia's Arab spring protesters were looking for and what they actually got. Political agency and political responsibility produced more responsive government, but more responsive government did not immediately put bread in anyone's mouth. Tunisia's new government therefore remains vulnerable to future threats and challenges like those that brought down Ben Ali—challenges based on the regime's failure to resolve deep-seated social economic problems.

What Went Right? Transition and Danger

From a constitutional or legal perspective, the most striking thing about the transition that followed Ben Ali's departure was its lack of formal rationality or justification drawn from political theory. There were no clear rules for what to do. And no one tried to draw them up, at least not right away.

First, after Ben Ali's flight from the country, his vice president, Mohammed Ghannouchi (not to be confused with the Islamist leader with whom he shared a last name), tried to salvage something of the old regime by assuming the post of prime minister and creating a national unity government. His government included members of some opposition parties but was dominated by members of Ben Ali's own party, the Rassemblement Constitutionnel Démocratique. The national unity government did not, however, include representatives from Ennahda, the Islamist party that remained banned. It was met by ongoing street protests across the country and lasted just six weeks. At the end of February 2011, the prime minister resigned, effectively acknowledging that he and his party were the primary targets of the protests.

During his brief period in office, the prime minister appointed a commission that was charged with planning constitutional reforms. It was led by a legal scholar, Yadh Ben Achour, who had been a cautious regime critic. As imagined initially, the commission might have proposed a new constitution on its own. Once it became clear that the public did not view the new government as legitimate, however, it followed that a commission appointed by that government would not have the legitimacy to make the reforms. To his credit, Ben Achour recognized this changing situation—and shifted the focus of his committee to proposing a broader framework for a democratic process of constitutional reform. The change was driven by political reality; yet acknowledging it was itself an important and prescient act of constitutional compromise.

Just before the prime minister resigned, it was announced that national elections would be held in the summer of 2011. This announcement created space for the appointment of a new prime minister, Beji Caid Essebsi, who was broadly seen as an interim caretaker until elections took place. Essebsi seemed like an obvious candidate for the caretaker role. Born in 1926, he was already eighty-four years old and thus did not seem likely to try consolidating power. He had been foreign minister twenty-five years earlier under Bourguiba and had since served only in minor, occasional roles under Ben Ali.

Essebsi would turn out not to be the footnote to Tunisian history that he was expected to become when he took the interim role. His transitional tenure extended longer than initially anticipated. Nevertheless, he did preside over a period that led to elections, which were delayed from the summer to the fall of 2011. Ennahda was legalized, setting the stage for its participation in electoral politics. A complex negotiation process, aided by the Ben Achour commission, led to the conclusion that the body to be elected would have the character of a constituent assembly empowered to draft a new constitution.

Notice that by electing a constituent assembly rather than a legislature, the transitional government managed to sidestep the thorny question of what legal or constitutional framework would authorize the election. In theory, a constituent assembly was itself a body that the people empowered to set the framework going forward. It was not, or was not meant to be, a body that would actually govern Tunisia.

Elections changed that expectation, however. Ennahda won a full 41 percent of the seats in the constituent assembly, enough for a comfortable plurality. For the first time, the Tunisian people could be said to have spoken formally, rather than through the more informal means of public protests. The elections meant that Ennahda would have to have some share in government and would not be limited to crafting a new constitution.

The solution to this potential problem was found in the constituent assembly. The first thing the assembly did was enact what came to be called the "mini-constitution": a document that not only set the ground rules for drafting and ratification but also established new quasi-legal norms that would enable the country to be governed while the process was ongoing. The mini-constitution inaugurated a distinctive Tunisian answer to the question of how to govern democratically in the absence of a democratically elected government: The constituent assembly would sit on alternating days as a drafting body and as a de facto national legislature.*

At the same time, Essebsi stepped down, and a coalition government, the "troika," was established. The national assembly elected a president, Moncef Marzouki, a liberal human rights advocate. He named Ennahda leader Hamadi Jebali as his prime minister. The speaker of the assembly, Mustapha Ben Jafar, was a leftist, secularist opposition politician. Together the troika

---

* In practice, different legislators focused on different subject-matter interests. Some became constitution experts; others only did ordinary legislation.

was poised to share power—with an understanding that Ennahda would be first among equals, commensurate with the election results.

The Assembly

Tunisia's constituent assembly was supposed to draft and ratify the constitution and then disband itself. The process took a full two years, significantly longer than was originally intended. During that period, the assembly repeatedly claimed its own inherent authority to extend its own life. Formally, this was a doubtful process. Practically, it was absolutely necessary.

The years 2012 and 2013 were tumultuous times for the constitutional process to be proceeding—for regional reasons as much as local ones. When the assembly was elected, the Muslim Brotherhood in nearby Egypt had not yet won the Egyptian elections. In neighboring Libya, Qaddafi had just been killed. By the time Tunisia's national assembly finally succeeded in ratifying a constitution, in January 2014, Morsi had been replaced by Sisi—and Libya was deep into the first phase of its civil war.

The Tunisian constitutional process took place in the shadow of the rest of the Arab spring—particularly the rapid rise and fall of democracy in Egypt. All the Tunisian participants, Islamists as well as secularists, were constantly evaluating their own situation, strategy, and prospects in relation to regional events. At every stage, overconfidence or breakdown was possible for the various actors. And yet at every stage, the potential for overreach and disaster was avoided.

The full story of how this happened deserves a book of its own, one that would chart the ebbs and flows of the Tunisian constitutional process through the eyes of the leading participants and representative members of the public.[5] That task is beyond my scope here. On half a dozen visits to the country to study the constitutional process and provide advice, I saw the process from the perspective of members of the constituent assembly, and in particular of those members who were willing to talk to me at length. No doubt my account is partly shaped by those interactions.

My goal is to highlight what seem to me the crucial moments of the constitutional process—those in which the relevant actors turned away from paths that would have led to failure. The constitutional process was, like any such process, profoundly political. Actors were interested in principles, to be sure—but in pursuit of those principles, the members of the constituent assembly and their organizations, like all elected politicians, used techniques of pressure politics. No viable political organization ever acts outside the framework of advancing its members' individual and collective goals. And yet one value ultimately trumped narrower interests and shaped decision making at crucial moments: the value of political responsibility, understood as the awareness that all Tunisians would have to live through the consequences of whatever decisions were made.

The first crossroads came in the aftermath of the constituent assembly elections in the fall of 2011. It was shaped by the plurality victory achieved by Ennahda. Many secular Tunisians experienced that victory as a frightening repudiation of their national self-conception as the most secular Arab country.[6] The Islamists of Ennahda, for their part, experienced the victory as a vindication of their belief that ordinary Tunisians remained profoundly connected to Islamic beliefs and values—and wanted to see those deployed in the realm of politics.

Both interpretations of Ennahda's plurality were overstated. To begin with, Islamic democratic parties won pluralities or majorities in every (even mildly) fair election held in the

Arabic-speaking world from Algeria in 1991 up to and including Tunisia's constituent assembly elections twenty years later. Tunisians on both sides of the political spectrum should have anticipated a similar result. Uncovering the reasons for that trend would have helped them understand why it was a mistake to assume that the public was rejecting secularism in favor of political Islam.

The basic causes of Islamist victories lay in that, in many of these elections, Islamists had tremendous first-mover advantages—particularly as elections took place against the backdrop of autocracy. Islamists had an inherently appealing message, combining nonspecific Islamic values with a commitment to democratic politics. In Tunisia as in other Arabic-speaking countries, decades of single-party police-state rule had eroded or destroyed most organized political parties.[7] When elections were declared, many existing parties had already been discredited by the perception that they had collaborated with the regime. New political parties take time to organize—while Islamist parties, such as Ennahda, had typically been banned, which gave them the imprimatur of not being regime sympathizers. This also ensured that, despite having high name recognition, they were not seen as corrupt, since they had had no share in the political power that would have allowed for corruption. In many instances, Ennahda included, Islamist political organizations had maintained secret, illegal cells throughout the country despite being banned. Together, these constituted enormous advantages in the first elections to be held in the aftermath of autocracy. In the case of Ennahda, the party leader, Rached el-Ghannouchi, was known from television appearances on Al Jazeera (even though he had been exiled), and the party very likely received financial support from sympathetic governments in the Gulf, such as Qatar.

What was more, Islamists seeking office in the two decades between 1991 and 2001 had hit upon an attractive, if rather abstract, political program that promised to reconcile Islam and democracy. No one, including the Islamic democrats, knew exactly what that would mean in practice. But where other political parties struggled to explain what they stood for, Islamic democrats had at their disposal a powerful rhetorical and ideological construct that would be difficult for most citizens of most Arabic-speaking countries to refute (at least, aspirationally). In embracing these guiding principles, Ennahda won its plurality in the constituent assembly elections simply because it was the Islamic democratic party on the ballot.

To both secularist opponents and Ennahda itself, the election results invited overreach. Opponents immediately had to consider the option of doing what the opponents and enemies of the Muslim Brotherhood did in Egypt: undertaking a sustained effort to use the state, as well as public pressure, to undermine and if possible bring down the Islamist government. Ennahda, for its part, faced the temptation of using its plurality in the constituent assembly to try to push through a constitution—and a resulting political order—that would entrench political Islam in Tunisia's form of government.

These competing temptations came into public view in February 2012, just when the constituent assembly was supposed to be getting down to business. Someone in Ennahda leaked a version of a draft constitution that had been circulating in party circles. The draft, following the norms of Islamic democratic constitutional thought, invoked shari'a as a basis for Tunisian law— which had not been the case under the Tunisian constitutions previously in force.

A series of public protests followed. The first, notably, were against the Islamization of the Tunisian constitution.[8] This was a watershed moment in the Tunisian constitutional process, and indeed in the region. It marked the first time in the post–Arab spring—and indeed, the first time in at least a generation—when spontaneous protests broke out in favor of secularism and against Islamism in an Arabic-speaking country. It was also the first major street protest in Tunisia after the democratic constituent assembly elections. As such, it made clear to Ennahda the risks associated with fully following its electoral success with policies that reflected the values it had espoused in winning it.

These anti-shariʿa protests were followed in early March by a significantly smaller (though not less intense) protest in favor of making shariʿa a key part of the constitution.[9] The speakers used terms familiar from Islamic democratic constitutional thought throughout the region, insisting on the sovereignty of God and the primacy of Islamic law in validating the legitimacy of the state. I was at this rally, and to me the air brimmed with confidence—confidence based on the protesters' commitment to principle and on Ennahda's electoral success.

Ennahda did not formally endorse this protest. But at least one senior Ennahda figure addressed the rally, using terms indistinguishable from those of the other speakers. This reflected what turned out to be an emerging split within the party. On one side were pragmatic, even liberal figures, most prominently Ghannouchi, the party leader, who wanted to avoid open conflict with the secularists. On the other side were more conservative Islamists, for whom the public commitment to shariʿa was more or less definitional. The conservatives also feared that softening on shariʿa would alienate a growing constituency of Salafi Islamists who were positioning themselves to the right of Ennahda and already staging small, separate public protests of their own.

At a dramatic private meeting of Ennahda's member-elected political leadership in late March 2012, these two views within the party came face-to-face. The leadership voted on a proposal to renounce formally any intent to invoke shari'a in the Tunisian constitution. According to sources present at the meeting, the first vote resulted in a slim majority in favor of retaining the demand for shari'a. Ghannouchi then told the assembled party leaders that he would resign from leadership of the party unless a revote was taken and a different result reached. The members voted again; this time, a slim majority agreed to adopt a measure declaring that Ennahda would not seek to have shari'a even mentioned in the constitution. Ghannouchi announced this policy at a press conference on March 26, 2012.[10]

Seen in terms of Islamic democratic constitutional politics, this renunciation was stunning. A party that had won a comfortable plurality in the constituent assembly was acknowledging that it would not seek to effectuate what most independent observers considered its most distinctive constitutional policy. The first major conflict in the Tunisian constitutional process had been averted.

The long-term constitutional effect of the renunciation was to shift the debate over the political theory of the Tunisian constitution. Now, all parties represented in the constituent assembly were advocating for some form of political liberalism, with some sort of distinction between religion and the state. Ultimately, Ghannouchi and Ennahda would argue for a liberal state that would protect religion from statist dominance and guarantee liberty for political actors to promote religious values in the public sphere. The constitution that would emerge would thus be not simply democratic but liberal-democratic.

What drove Ennahda's decision was, above all, the recognition that the question of shari'a could have split the public and constituent assembly, thus blocking the process of constitution making before it could really begin. The decision was realistic and pragmatic—and reflected a profound sense of political responsibility. Instead of insisting that its electoral plurality authorized the party to dictate policy, Ennahda learned the first and most important lesson of constitution making: that a vocal and empowered faction must be respected, even if it is an electoral minority. In a constitution-making process, winning a plurality of votes does not mean getting everything you want.

It would be difficult to think of a point on which there was starker contrast between Ennahda and the Egyptian Muslim Brotherhood, which repeatedly failed to learn this basic lesson. Indeed, the Muslim Brotherhood constitution, influenced partly by the pressure of Egyptian Salafis, went even further than the preexisting Egyptian constitution in enshrining shari'a, while insisting that its electoral pluralities and majorities gave it the right to adopt the constitutional policies it wanted. This was the opposite of political responsibility. Morsi and his government did not think about the consequences of their enactments for all Egyptians—nor did they seek consensus.

Ghannouchi was helped in reaching his compromise position by ideological flexibility. His own intellectual journey had drawn him in the direction of political liberalism, particularly a Lockean rejection of religious coercion. Because Ghannouchi rejected the idea that the state could impose shari'a, he was able to redefine the goals of Islamic constitutionalism away from enshrining shari'a and toward protecting religion from the state. There can be little doubt that Tunisia had good fortune in having a leader of Ghannouchi's intellect, character, and leadership, all of which were absent in the Egyptian Muslim Brotherhood and particularly in Morsi.

A further advantage that Tunisia possessed was a political culture highly focused on the value of consensus. Consensus and its variants were constantly invoked by leaders both inside and outside the constituent assembly, and identified almost ritually as a distinctive Tunisian ideal. As the Tunisian scholar and activist Nadia Marzouki has put it, "a number of related concepts [were] front and center: consensus (*ijma'*), alliance (*tahaluf*), cooperation (*ta'awun*), union (*ittihad*), deal (*safaqa*), pact (*ittifaq*), contract (*'aqd*), negotiation (*tafawud*), dialogue (*hiwar*), moderation (*i'tidal*), solidarity (*tadamun*) and forgiveness (*tasamuh*)."[11]

Tracing the sources of political self-conception is never simple. It seems possible that the value of consensus was produced by Habib Bourguiba's regime, as a mechanism for achieving social and political control.[12] Still, whatever its origins, there are worse values for a polity to have, when trying to produce a new constitution, than an incompletely theorized and non-rational commitment to getting along. Despite the fact that political consensus can suppress dissent, it has the virtue of encouraging the political elite to engage in an iterative process of negotiation—which takes place against the backdrop of a feeling that failure to reach consensus could produce disaster.

The Crisis

Averting the first potential disaster of the constitutional process was, however, no guarantee of ultimate success. Although the drafting of constitutional provisions continued at a slow but steady pace, the combination of internal pressures with the external meltdown of the Egyptian experiment in democracy produced a further crisis in 2013.

Two assassinations heralded the Tunisian crisis: that of Chokri Belaid in February 2013 and Mohammed Brahmi in July. Both men were leftist Arab nationalists, former critics of the Ben Ali regime who were committed to the formation of secularist government. Belaid was a leader of a small party called the Democratic Patriots' Unified Party that had just one seat in the constituent assembly, occupied by someone else. Brahmi served in the assembly as one of just two delegates representing a party called the People's Movement. While alive, neither was a central figure in Tunisia's post–Arab spring politics. Yet given the climate, their deaths stood for something much greater, namely the threat to secularism and socialism associated with the rise of Islamic politics.

The probable assassin or assassins (the same gun was allegedly used in both cases) were not supporters of Ennahda but Salafi-jihadis who likely sought to weaken Ennahda by creating instability. If that was indeed the strategy, it worked. After Belaid's assassination, public protests by secularists sharply criticized Ennahda. The legitimacy of the troika government was thrown into question, as the Islamic democratic party was associated in the public mind with violence against secularists.

Seeking a solution after the first assassination, the Ennahda prime minister, Hamadi Jebali, offered his resignation. The act had important symbolic significance. One of the longtime worries about the election of Islamist government was that it would lead to "one man, one vote, one time"—the entrenchment of power. Jebali's resignation was intended to signal that the Islamists were open to leaving office, just as they had been open to sharing power when initially elected.

Within Ennahda, there was serious doubt about whether it was a good idea for the party to withdraw from government in response to an event that it denounced and claimed to have no part in. In particular, some party members worried that once out of government, despite enjoying an electoral plurality, Ennahda would not be allowed back. They feared a de facto secularist coup against them. Jebali's detractors in Ennahda also suggested that he was engaged in a personalized publicity stunt, designed to put him in position for an eventual presidential run.

After Jebali's resignation, another Ennahda politician, Ali Laarayedh—a former dissident who had gone from being tortured in prison under Ben Ali to serving as minister of justice—became prime minister. His new government appointed more technocratic ministers and had less representation from Ennahda. This attempt at compromise might have worked had it not been for the Brahmi assassination, which triggered new anti-Ennahda protests and made clear to the party's leadership that it must take seriously the possibility that Ennahda could be suppressed as was happening to the Brotherhood in Egypt.

It was now August 2013. In Egypt, Sisi had removed Morsi from office, and the understanding of everyone in the Tunisian political scene was that regional energy had now turned definitively against the Islamists. The possibility of a democratic breakdown was immediate. Tunisia was entering the crucible of its democratic transition.

The unlikely figure who emerged as a possible Sisi at this juncture was Beji Caid Essebsi, now eighty-six, who had honorably served as interim prime minister after the revolution and before the constituent assembly elections, then stepped down as part of the transition. When I met Essebsi in his opulent living room, it seemed almost inconceivable to me that this rather grand epitome of old-line, secular Arab nationalism could reemerge into a position of power in Tunisian politics. On the surface, Essebsi seemed to stand for everything the Arab spring had come to wash away.

Yet Essebsi had been hard at work crafting a coalition of secularists and other mainstream Tunisians who wanted to resist an Islamist future for the state. Known as Nidaa Tounes (the Call of Tunisia), the party was nakedly a vehicle for Essebsi to become president. Yet for secularists who wanted to ensure that they would elect the president of Tunisia after the ratification of the constitution, that was enough. Essebsi possessed authority, name recognition, and seriousness that no other secularist candidate could muster. He also naturally attracted both elites and rank and file from the Ben Ali era, who saw the party as the best route to restoring their previous privileges.

In the tense weeks that followed, Essebsi and his Nidaa Tounes became central players in negotiating the fate of the country— despite not having run for office in the elections or holding any seats in the constituent assembly. On the other side of the negotiations was Ennahda, which had won and still held the plurality in the assembly but whose tenuous hold on the power it shared within the troika government left it in serious jeopardy. The model of Egypt was now first and foremost in everyone's mind, further weakening Ennahda's position.

Left to their own devices, Ennahda and Nidaa Tounes might well have failed to reach a negotiated solution. Ennahda had a claim to democratic legitimacy but rapidly shrinking actual sway. Nidaa Tounes had little claim to democratic legitimacy but held the implicit threat of a Sisi-style return to power with the acquiescence or assistance of Tunisian intelligence services and the military. As we know from the example of Egypt, this was not a promising starting position for successfully negotiating a solution for sharing power.

But Tunisia had something that Egypt lacked: an evolved set of functioning civil society institutions, all of which had a stake in continued stability—and which had, perhaps more importantly, a stake in avoiding a return to autocracy. The four most influential were the labor union (Union générale tunisienne du travail [UGTT]), which had a claim to have sparked the Arab spring in the first place with public strikes;[13] an employers' union (Union tunisienne de l'industrie, du commerce et de l'artisanat [UTICA]), something like a cartel with representation from every industry except tourism and the financial sector; the leading human rights association (Ligue tunisienne des droits de l'homme [LTDH]); and the national lawyers' association. Together, with the UGTT in the lead, the quartet formed what came to be called the "national dialogue"—essentially a framework for a multiparty negotiation, designed to break what might otherwise have been a direct standoff between Ennahda and Nidaa Tounes.

Civil Society and Its Discontents

Why did Tunisia have a civil society capable of playing a crucial political role when most other post–Arab spring states did not? Similar organizations to those that made up the quartet existed in nearly every Arab presidential republic. In most, however, the organizations had come to be controlled by the apparatus of the state and the presidential party.[14] In Iraq, for example—admittedly an extreme case—the so-called civil society institutions that existed under Saddam were a kind of Potemkin village of pseudo-civil society. The Iraqi national lawyers' association, to choose an institution I saw in action firsthand, had come to be controlled by the personal lawyer for one of Saddam's sons—and was nothing more than a fiefdom within the broader Ba'th Party domains.[15]

The Tunisian difference lay in the particular form of presidential autocracy that had existed under Bourguiba and persisted under Ben Ali. In the absence of oil wealth controlled by the government or significant direct foreign aid, presidential rule had to be consolidated partly via public acquiescence, not only by the tools of totalitarian oppression. The civil society institutions facilitated the production of the same social consensus of which Tunisians were later to become so proud. Naturally, Bourguiba and Ben Ali both tried to take control of the UGTT; and at various points in the history of the union, they sometimes appeared to have succeeded.[16] But complete suppression of the labor union's representative function was never possible and never fully accomplished in the way it was in most other autocratic Arab dictatorships. The reason was that, even under Ben Ali's regime, the labor union and an employers' union were necessary for helping the autocratic government facilitate social peace.[17] Thus the possibility of episodic labor strikes was a price the government was willing to pay in order to preserve order and control.

Similarly, Ben Ali tried repeatedly—and with partial success—to install regime-loyal leadership at the LTDH.[18] Yet he never took the path of trying to suppress the human rights group altogether, presumably because he perceived legitimacy gains from its continued operation and did not want to pay the price of appearing to be afraid of its continued existence. Consequently, the human rights and lawyers' associations under the old regime did not so much guarantee human rights or the independence of the legal system as provide forums for negotiating rights and legal authority in complex interaction with the presidency and the state.[19]

In a sense, then, in helping broker the national dialogue, the quartet of civil society institutions was continuing the organizations' accustomed role of facilitating a consensual social order. A key difference was that, under presidential autocracy, these institutions were necessarily subordinate to the threat of state power. Now, the threat was rather the weakening or dissolution of the state in the wake of the conflict emerging between Ennahda and Nidaa Tounes. Neither labor nor industry wanted a return to presidential dictatorship, in which their power would have been at best returned to the status quo ante. What they wanted was to exert new and greater influence on the Tunisian state.

The good news is that, with the help of the quartet, Nidaa Tounes and Ennahda reached a grand bargain.[20] The troika government stepped down. The new constitution that had been drafted gradually by the constituent assembly since the revolution was at length ratified. The document adopted roughly the French form of "semi-presidentialism," in which the president is entrusted with foreign affairs and security power, and the parliamentary prime minister with administrative and legislative authority. Ennahda announced it would not officially endorse any one presidential candidate in upcoming elections, thus implicitly standing aside to enable Essebsi's candidacy, despite their ideological differences. In turn, Essebsi pledged to uphold the principles of the constitution, which Ennahda hoped would block Essebsi from suppressing the party or democratic politics in general.

The deal held. Essebsi was elected president. In the fall of 2014, Nidaa Tounes won a plurality in legislative elections, gaining eighty seats to Ennahda's sixty-nine. Essebsi took no overt steps to suppress Ennahda. This marked the first time there had been a democratic transition of political parties in modern Arab history. The Tunisian consensus model worked, and Tunisia became the first functioning democracy in the Arabic-speaking world. For its contribution to the process, the quartet was awarded the Nobel Peace Prize in 2015. Nidaa Tounes and Ennahda entered into an alliance that lasted until the fall of 2018.[21] Essebsi lived until July 2019, when he died peacefully in office at the age of ninety-two, widely hailed as a hero, even by Ennahda supporters who had feared he would attempt to suppress their party.

The bad news hidden in this uplifting story—at least, potentially—is that by brokering the deal between Nidaa Tounes and Ennahda, the quartet got what its members most wanted: an effective guarantee of rough continuity in the economic structure of the state rather than economic reforms. This was not a formal guarantee. No written promises were made to any of the civil society organizations. Rather, by demonstrating their power through the national dialogue process, those institutions—and in particular both the labor union and the employers' association—assured that the government that emerged would not try to challenge them with respect to their particular interests.[22]

In practice, this has meant, for example, that the government of Tunisia has not meaningfully reduced public sector employment. This would have angered the labor union, many of whose members are public employees.[23] Similarly, Tunisia has not undertaken institutional reforms of the kind that would have made entrepreneurship a more attractive or viable option for a broader swath of the population. The employers' union, functioning as a cartel of business owners, has a natural economic interest in maintaining the high barriers to entry that already exist for starting new businesses in the country.

The direct or implicit influence of the civil society institutions is not the only factor explaining the slowness of economic reform in Tunisia. Probably no government would want to risk worsening the unemployment that fed the 2011 uprising. As it is, unemployment is the most common spark of ongoing protests in the country.

The very structure of consensus government is another major cause of stasis. With neither major party outside government, the incentive to make fundamental change is reduced, because both parties could claim credit for success. True, the danger of failed reform is modestly reduced when the major parties are in coalition. But given the possibility that new external parties could be created when there is substantial public dissatisfaction with the existing government, the incentives against risk-taking in government mostly outweigh those of reform and experimentation.

In other words, the very consensus structures that helped Tunisia avoid the fate of Egypt have created conditions in which the underlying economic causes that sparked the Arab spring protests have not been addressed. Unemployment is lower than it was in 2010–11, but that seems to be the result of cyclical trends, neither a result of new government policy nor a signal of improved economic outlook. As of this writing, there does not seem to be a political constellation on the horizon likely to drive substantial reform in the future.

This brings us to the financial sector and its role in sustaining Tunisia's economy in its current unreformed state. According to the French political economist Béatrice Hibou, prerevolutionary Tunisia was characterized by a deep structure of "bad debt." In essence, Hibou has argued, foreign and international financial institutions loaned money to Tunisian state financial institutions as well as some private sector banks on the theory that Tunisia was reforming and liberalizing its economy. The state then guided the distribution of these loans in a pattern designed to maintain its political stability rather than to invest in the entrepreneurs and businesses most likely to succeed. Effective reform did not occur, and the image of Tunisia as an economic model (or "miracle") was a fiction. Unsurprisingly, a high percentage of the loans ended in default; but in the meantime, the flow of capital functioned as a kind of rent that kept the economy afloat. Hibou refers to the whole unstable arrangement as a mechanism of "reforms in perpetuity."[24]

If Hibou is right, one major consequence of the revolution—not intended but also not coincidental—is that the Tunisian state has developed a new kind of reform-based argument that it can make in international financial circles in favor of continued infusions of capital. Now that Tunisia can present itself as a model of democracy, the survival of the state in its democratic form becomes an independent reason to justify new loans, as guarantors of stability. The new democratic state can be expected to distribute the largesse of those loans in somewhat new ways, relative to the ancien régime. But democracy in itself cannot guarantee a more economically efficient distribution—merely a distribution that reflects a different array of state interests. People who were dependent on the old state for patronage will still be dependent on the new one.

The political economy of the new Tunisia may therefore turn out to have a great deal in common with the old. Foreign states and international financial institutions continue to make "investments" in the form of capital and credit. Those capital flows help shore up the existing state and manage, to a degree, the continuance of social peace. Yet the underlying economic structure remains unstable and perhaps even unsustainable over the long term. Tunisia's economy still lacks a significant unique advantage for production or service delivery. And the dream of entrepreneurship remains as far off as ever for most ordinary Tunisians, even though there is foreign capital enough to fund start-ups— if only entrepreneurs were able to access it.

Mismatch and Democracy

The upshot of this failure of reform is that there appears to be a significant gap between what brought Tunisians to the streets to start the Arab spring and what Tunisians have actually gained as a result of their revolution. Recall that "dignity"— karama—was a watchword of the Tunisian revolution. Tunisians even named the revolution "the dignity revolution," preferring this over the "Jasmine revolution," which was used by some outsiders. Sadly, dignity in its full meaning has not been delivered.

The call for dignity that characterized the revolution was first and foremost a call for the economic dignity that comes with employment and a living wage. No doubt it was also a call for respectful treatment by state officials who take rights seriously. But the former element predominated.

That aspect—economic dignity derived from a stable economy and predictable employment at a living wage—remains unaddressed by the revolution. Given the structure of consensus politics and the inherent difficulty of structural economic reform, it may well remain so for the foreseeable future. Tunisian revolutionaries sought economic reform, and instead they got constitutional government.

To be sure, the liberal-democratic constitutional state that did emerge from the revolution does confer dignity of the second, rights-based type. A state governed by law and an elected government answerable to the population will, in general, do a better job of treating its citizens with respect and honoring their fundamental rights than does a dictatorship. Mohamed Bouazizi would today have a better chance than before the revolution of avoiding the treatment that pushed him to the brink of suicide, namely police abuse and the confiscation of his stock of fruit. This improvement must not be ignored or gainsaid. It constitutes the bulk of what most Western liberal democrats consider the great desideratum of government.

Yet the dire economic conditions under which Bouazizi lived and died were presumably more central to his exhaustion and despair—and to the subsequent revolution—than the mistreatment he faced. A polity that treats its citizens with decency but cannot deliver a sustainable economic system is vulnerable to a powerful sense of illegitimacy. In the current historical moment, at least, such a state seems much more vulnerable than a state like China, which in recent decades has provided hugely improved economic well-being without granting its citizens liberal rights.

That does not mean the Tunisian constitutional revolution is doomed. For one thing, liberal democracy allows constitutionally protected space for public protests. Those have abounded in Tunisia, including in the years since the constitution was ratified and government got down to the business of governing. Most of the protests in Tunisia focus on the economy. In January 2018, more than twenty cities across the country saw major protests over rising prices, some of them violent.[25] In January 2019, 670,000 people joined in a general strike called by the labor union.[26]

In a liberal democracy, the protests need not translate into demands for a new regime. Tunisians now understand that democracy offers no inherent answer to economic troubles. But that means they also understand that a return to autocracy would not solve those troubles either. Thus protests that challenge the government need not challenge the structure of constitutional democracy itself.

This is an important feature of political responsibility in a successful democracy. In an autocracy, people may imagine they can improve their lot by overthrowing both the government and the type of regime, as happened in the Arab spring. In a democracy, however, people exercising political responsibility know that they cannot improve matters by overthrowing themselves. The Egyptian people, expressing their collective will but not a sense of responsibility, did in fact invite the overthrow of their own democracy. The Tunisian people, acting on the principle that they must take responsibility for their own fate, are very unlikely to bring about the overthrow of their own democratic authority—at least, not by choice.

The reason is that Tunisians cannot and do not fantasize that someone or something else will save them—not a dictator, not a foreign state, and not Islam itself. Political responsibility means recognizing that help cannot come from the outside but rather from within. If Tunisians wreck their constitutional democracy, no one else will save them. That knowledge should help protect them from the temptation to make the Egyptian choice of throwing self-government away.

Part of accepting political responsibility is admitting that constitutional democracy is not perfect or ideal but just the least-bad option. Preserving it is hard work. Often, its advantages do not seem obvious or tangible. Sometimes, the benefits do not even seem capable of outweighing the costs. Yet the inchoate benefit of constitutional democracy, the advantage that the people of Tunisia still seem to value above all, is the exercise of genuine self-government.

Conclusion: The Lessons of Tunisia and the Meaning of Tragedy

Taken on its own, the story of Tunisia is not a tragedy but a moving chapter in both the inspirational and quotidian realities of self-government. To have created the first functioning Arab democracy is a generational, historic achievement. Doing so would have been difficult even under the best of circumstances. Accomplishing democracy while the rest of the Arab spring countries backed into autocracy, or worse, looks like something of a miracle.

As I have argued, the keys to that epochal achievement were compromise and consensus, tools deployed against the backdrop of political responsibility. The reality of such realism is that there are limits to what a compromise can include. In Tunisia, the consensus favored by the national unity government maintained and enhanced preexisting incentives against risky structural transformation. And the productive role of civil society in crafting compromise simultaneously entrenched the power of certain economic actors, who continue to resist reform.

But these are ordinary problems for an ordinary democratic polity. To have crafted and (so far) sustained such a polity is itself well worth celebrating. Seen from this perspective, the lesson of Tunisia is that an Arabic-speaking country can successfully manage the transition from autocracy to democracy. What happened in Tunisia could happen elsewhere.

Skeptics sometimes object that the success of democracy in Tunisia could never figure as a model for other Arabic-speaking countries. Tunisia is uniquely small, they say. It is denominationally, ethnically, and linguistically homogeneous—at least, after the coercive Arabization of the Amazigh (Berber) population and the emigration of the Jews.[27] Tunisia is also discounted as a model because of its secularism, its high degree of education and literacy, and its cultural connections to France.

The trouble with these deflationary arguments is that Tunisia already did serve as a model for other Arab countries. Its protests and the departure of Ben Ali sparked the Arab spring, a regional phenomenon that spanned larger, less homogeneous states with more (and more radical) local Islamism. If Tunisia could inspire Arab peoples to seek self-determination and regime change, why could it not eventually inspire the Arab world to adopt constitutional democracy as a solution to the exercise of self-governing politics?

With respect to political Islam, the Tunisian example reveals yet a different direction than the failure of the Egyptian Muslim

Brotherhood and of the Islamic State. Ennahda did not fail, but it evolved under pressure into a party form that was not Islamist in that it no longer offers Islam as "the solution" to all the problems of politics. By comparing itself to a Christian democratic party in Europe, Ennahda has embraced a liberal version of Islamic politics—liberal in its commitment to some separation of state from religion and also to the protection of religious politics from secularist state intervention. Attractive as this vision is, it remains to be seen whether it will catch on and achieve popularity even in Tunisia, to say nothing of the rest of the Arabic-speaking world. Seen in these terms, Ennahda in its own way also demonstrates the end of political Islam in the era of the Arab winter, albeit an ending reached not through suppression but through internal evolution.

When viewed as a reflection of this book's central theme of the meaning of political action, Tunisia demonstrates the power of what can go right—and thus highlights the tragedy of what can happen when the action goes wrong. The sense of tragedy sharpened by the Tunisian example is not that what happened there was unique. Rather, the tragedy is that what happened there could have happened elsewhere, and yet did not. Tunisia demonstrates that there was nothing inevitable about Egypt's reembrace of autocracy. The Muslim Brotherhood there could have built coalitions; Egypt's liberals could have brokered compromise between old-regime loyalists and the Morsi government; the military could have retained an influential position in society without running the state.

Tunisia also suggests that the collapse of Syria need not have been inevitable either. In Syria, no one exercised political responsibility—because no one accepted that the fate of Syrians rested ultimately in Syrian hands. The Sunnis who rose up against Bashar did not think seriously about how they could reach out to the 'Alawi community, manage their fears, and hence draw them away from supporting Bashar. Once the regime's response caused the uprising to turn violent, the Sunnis hoped and expected that outsiders, especially the old and new imperial powers of the West, would intervene from the air and give them victory by taking out the dictator—further avoiding direct responsibility.

As for Bashar and his regime, they, too, failed to demonstrate political responsibility. Devastating their opponents meant ethnically cleansing their own country of large swaths of its Sunni population. No doubt the Ba'th regime saw this as necessary for survival; but the survival of the regime came at the expense of the survival of the country, which today seems barely viable. The regime was therefore not taking responsibility for the safety of the society that it purported to govern. Instead of seeking a power-sharing arrangement that might have prolonged the survival of his regime, Bashar sought the total defeat of his rivals.

Once total war began, the regime, as much as the rebels, looked outside the country for a determinative solution. It relied on Iran, on its proxy militia of Lebanese Hezbollah, and eventually on Russian air support to win and reestablish control. Far from considering that no one would come to his aid, Bashar assumed—correctly, it turned out—that ultimate responsibility for Syria would be taken by other powers, regional and neo-imperial.

Had Syrians acted like Tunisians and taken responsibility for the fate of their country, it would still have been extraordinarily difficult to find a solution. But massive death and war might have been averted, or at least mitigated. The state might not have lost all authority over much of the country. And the Islamic State might not have filled the vacuum with its revolutionary-revivalist dystopia.

A similar analysis could be applied to Libya and Yemen, the other exemplars of post–Arab spring civil war. Internecine struggle could not have been avoided altogether. But the exercise of political responsibility could have made things far better in both countries, and perhaps the worst of what did happen could have been avoided.

Tunisia thus illuminates the contours of the tragedy that is the Arab winter. It is tragic enough that, after the noble aspirations of the Arab spring, the Egyptian people used their collective agency to renounce collective agency. It is tragic enough that Syrians' efforts to exercise the power of collective self-determination led them into brutal civil war. It is tragic enough that the Islamic State's attempt to create an independent, postcolonial polity was inextricably intertwined with murder and rape.

It is more tragic still that none of this was inevitable, as the contrasting narrative in Tunisia shows. The appeal of the value of political self-determination lies in the ideal of human free will. Tunisia helps remind us that the freedom of human will is real, at least when it comes to politics. That makes the successful exercise of political action heroic; and it turns the failures of human politics into nearly unbearable triggers of terror and pity.

CATHARSIS?

As I was preparing this volume for publication, in the spring of 2019, two sets of roughly simultaneous events occurred that seemed very much like afterimages of the Arab spring. First in Algeria and then in Sudan, both countries where 2011 protests failed to make a big impact, large crowds gathered to protest unfree elections that promised to keep in place two old, longstanding dictators, Abdelaziz Bouteflika and Omar al-Bashir. Both leaders resisted for a time, but the protests persisted. Soon enough Bouteflika resigned, and Bashir was removed by the Sudanese military. The people, it seemed, had gotten what they wanted—at least in the moment.

It is too soon to say definitively what will follow the removal of these leaders. Yet in both cases the hopeful tone of the protesters must be measured against the great probability that military regimes will use the protests as a means to replace the old autocratic rulers with younger ones, thus solving the transition problem that characteristically plagues military-backed dictatorial regimes. That, after all, is the descriptive-cynical account of what ultimately happened in Egypt. In neither Algeria nor Sudan does the military seem in jeopardy of being replaced as the dominant guarantor of political authority in the state. Even civil war cannot be ruled out, although its likelihood in both places is lessened (painfully, to be sure) by the fact that Algeria and Sudan have already undergone relatively recent civil wars, Algeria's between 1991 and 1999, and Sudan's from 1983 to 2005.

What do these belated mini Arab springs mean, taking place as they are in the depths of the Arab winter? The first lesson is surely that the original Arab spring protests still possess resonance and the power of example—notwithstanding the tragic consequences that followed in most of the places where they occurred. The Algerian and Sudanese protesters were in an important sense following a script that was familiar to them from the events of eight years before. Their songs and slogans were their own, but the precedent for creative use of songs and slogans in public protests to remove dictators had been set in 2011. It was still strong. And it still worked to remove the dictators from power.

A second lesson is that genuine, optimistic political action to change government remains possible in the Arabic-speaking world, even in the face of the experience of tragic failure. That is, the noble aspiration of the people to take charge of their own political destiny has not been eliminated or destroyed, despite the knowledge that failure is not merely possible but probable. Like the Arab spring protesters before them, the protesters in Sudan and Algeria were acting on their own, not in the shadow of empire nor against it. There is something uplifting about this persistence of hopeful commitment to autonomous political action, something especially moving in the light of the very tragedy this book has depicted.

The third lesson is more sober: the 2019 protests carry ennobling political meaning even if they ultimately fail to produce significant improvements in the lives of the peoples of Algeria and Sudan. Realism demands the recognition that Algeria and

Sudan have more in common with Egypt and even perhaps Libya and Syria than with Tunisia. The delicate conditions that can nurture the emergence of democratic constitutional government do not appear to obtain in either place. And if the script of the Arab spring was available to the protesters, the script of the Arab winter is available to the military authorities. Continued dictatorship is the most probable result; yet the struggle to do better still carries profound meaning.

In considering these afterimages of spring-in-winter, I am really asking: What comes after tragedy? Aristotle famously used the Greek word "catharsis" to capture the experience of the tragedy's observer. A catharsis, according to the weight of scholarly interpretation, is a purging or a purgation—an inner experience that transcends the emotions of terror and pity and turns them into something cleansing. In this much-analyzed picture, tragedy functions as a shaper of the viewer's internal cognitive and emotional state. It reflects that strand in Aristotle's thinking that sees the greatest human accomplishment as *theoria*, the speculative use of the mind to achieve what is most divine about us.

But the Arabic reception of Aristotle's conception of tragedy is, famously, different. Ibn Rushd, the great medieval commentator on Aristotle, interpreted tragedy and comedy through the filter of the very different Arabic literary genres of blame and praise poetry, in which the poet faults or idealizes an enemy or a patron. This reading—or perhaps misprision—is explored by Jorge Luis Borges in his poignant and beautiful orientalist story, "La busca de Averroes" ("Averroes's Search").

As Ibn Rushd has it, tragic catharsis "makes souls become tender and prompts them to accept the virtues."[1] This version of catharsis starts inwardly, with the preparation of the soul taking place through the experience of observing tragedy. But it moves outward, to the embrace of character virtues that can then be expressed through actual human action.

In this way, the catharsis of the Arabic Aristotle invokes a different, competing strand of Aristotelian thought—a strand that sees not reflection but the doing of politics as the highest form of human flourishing. The point of tragedy, in this vision, is to offer inspiration for the exercise of virtue, including political virtue. Tragedy can thus be made to have a practical, forward-looking purpose. It can lead us to do better.

The lessons in virtue that tragedy can teach are not pedagogically simple. There is no handbook for successful self-determination. Human conditions and circumstances vary too widely, as Aristotle noted. No single political or constitutional solution will fit every polity.

Yet tragedy seen through the lens of the Arabic Aristotelian tradition may nonetheless guide us toward political virtue, by its capacity to help us do better in the future. Bleak as circumstances are now for Arab politics, there will be changes. New possibilities will eventually emerge. The current winter may last a generation or more. But after the winter—and from its depths—always comes another spring.

ACKNOWLEDGMENTS

The impetus for the research that led to this book came from Duncan Pickard, who appeared in my office unannounced in the fall of 2011 and told me I had to come to Tunisia to study the constitutional process there and offer what help I could. I took Duncan's direction and through him came to meet an extraordinary range of Tunisian participants in their constituent assembly. I am deeply grateful to Duncan. I could not have written this book without him.

Our travel and research were supported by a generous grant from the Smith-Richardson Foundation, administered first by the Atlantic Council and then with great enthusiasm by Peter Bergen and the New America Foundation. For excellent research assistance I am grateful to Gal Koplewitz, Zoe Simon, Nate Orbach, Medha Gargeya, and Samarth Desai. My colleague and friend Jill Goldenziel read the manuscript and commented extensively, as she has generously done for every book I've written. As usual her comments improved my work tremendously, although my errors and omissions remain very much my own.

The Kamel Center at the Yale Law School, directed by Owen M. Fiss and Anthony Kronman, twice invited me to present early versions of the argument here: as the Dallah al-Baraka lecture, "Fall of the Arab Spring," in October 2013; and then in a series of three lectures titled "Arab Winter," delivered in September and October 2017. I am grateful to the participants in the conversations that followed all these lectures. My intellectual and other debts to my teachers Owen and Tony are of the kind that can only be acknowledged, never repaid.

NOTES

Preface

1. Seth G. Jones, "The Mirage of the Arab Spring," *Foreign Affairs*, January/February 2013, https://www.foreignaffairs.com/articles/syria/2012-12-03/mirage-arab -spring; Steven A. Cook, *False Dawn: Protest, Democracy, and Violence in the Middle East* (New York: Oxford University Press, 2017).

2. Shadi Hamid, *Islamic Exceptionalism: How the Struggle over Islam Is Reshaping the World* (New York: St. Martin's Press, 2016).

3. My argument differs radically from that of Hamid Dabashi, *The Arab Spring: The End of Postcolonialism* (Chicago: University of Chicago Press for Zed Books, 2012), written in the first euphoric moments of the Arab spring. There was no "permanent revolutionary moment" that emerged from the Arab spring, and if there was, its consequences were often malign rather than positive. Nevertheless the book reflects some initial recognition that the events of the Arab spring marked a distinctive new era of Arab history in relation to traditional discourses of colonialism and imperialism.

4. For an expansive treatment of this definition, see Noah Feldman, *The Fall and Rise of the Islamic State* (Princeton: Princeton University Press, 2012), 105–46.

5. See, e.g., Belqis Al-Sowaidi, Felix Banda, and Arwa Mansour, "Doing Politics in the Recent Arab Uprisings: Towards a Political Discourse Analysis of the Arab Spring Slogans," *Journal of Asian and African Studies* 52, no. 5 (2017): 621–45; F. A. Al-Haq and A. Hussein, "The Slogans of the Tunisian and Egyptian Revolutions," in *42nd Colloquium on African Languages and Linguistics (CALL), Leiden, The Netherlands, 27–29 August 2012* (Leiden: Leiden University Centre for Linguistics, 2012); M. Lahlali, "The Discourse of Egyptian Slogans: From 'Long Live Sir' to 'Down with the Dictator,'" *Journal of Arab Media and Society* 19 (2014): 1–14.

6. For a journalist's first draft of historical overview, see, e.g., Robert F. Worth, *A Rage for Order: The Middle East in Turmoil, From Tahrir Square to ISIS* (New York: Farrar, Straus and Giroux, 2016). For excellent analytic political science, see, e.g., Jason Brownlee, Tarek Masoud, and Andrew Reynolds, *The Arab Spring: Pathways of Repression and Reform* (Oxford: Oxford University Press, 2015).

7. Hannah Arendt, *On Revolution* (New York: Penguin Books, 1963).

8. Hannah Arendt, *The Human Condition* (Chicago: University of Chicago Press, 1958), 7.

9. Ibid.

10. Ibid., 9.

11. Arendt, *On Revolution*, 275.

12. Lucy Crane, "Hannah Arendt on the Principles of Political Action," *European Journal of Political Theory* 1 (2015): 55.

13. Arendt, *The Human Condition*, 205–6.

14. Noah Feldman, *After Jihad: America and the Struggle for Islamic Democracy* (New York: Farrar, Straus and Giroux, 2003).

15. Noah Feldman, *What We Owe Iraq: War and the Ethics of Nation-Building* (Princeton: Princeton University Press, 2004).

16. Feldman, *Fall and Rise of the Islamic State*.

17. On different theories of tragedy, see Raymond Williams, *Modern Tragedy* (Peterborough, Ontario: Broadview Press, 1966); W. H. Auden, "The Globe," in *The Dyer's Hand and Other Essays* (New York: Vintage International, 1990), 174–76. See also Clifford Leech, *Tragedy* (London: Methuen & Co., 1969), 38–41; Harold Osborne, "The Concept of Tragedy," *British Journal of Aesthetics* 15, no. 4 (1975): 287–93, 289.

18. Note that Aristotle equivocates with respect to predetermination, allowing for *either* necessity *or* probability: "With character, precisely as in the structure of events, one should always seek *necessity or probability*—so that for such a person to say or do such things is *necessary or probable*, and the sequence of events is also *necessary or probable*." *Poetics*, 1454a, 32–36, Loeb Classical Library, ed. and trans. Stephen Halliwell (Cambridge, MA: Harvard University Press, 1995), emphasis added.

Chapter 1: The People Want

1. Compare Adeed Dawisha, *Arab Nationalism in the Twentieth Century: From Triumph to Despair*, new ed. (Princeton: Princeton University Press, 2016), 146.

2. Abu al-Qasim al-Shabbi or Aboul-Qacem Echebbi (1909–1934), "Idha al-sha'b yawman arada hayat," also called "Iradat al-hayat," roughly, "the will to live."

3. One important difference is oil wealth. As has been frequently noted, regimes fell mostly in non-oil-producing countries, with the exception of Libya, where the United States and NATO brought down Qaddafi. See, as examples, Brownlee, Masoud, and Reynolds, *The Arab Spring*, 54; Leif Wenar, *Blood Oil: Tyrants, Violence, and the Rules that Run the World* (Oxford: Oxford University Press, 2016), 31–32. Of course Syria turned out also to be an exception in the other direction: its regime survived despite no oil wealth. No monarchy collapsed as the result of the Arab spring. The age and health of the dictator also turned out to be important factors.

4. On the use of Arabic language to produce transnational discourse in the Arab spring slogans, see Nazir Nader Harb Michel, *"Irhal!": The Role of Language in the*

Arab Spring (master's thesis, Georgetown University, 2013), https://repository.library
.georgetown.edu/bitstream/handle/10822/707400/HarbMichel_georgetown
_0076M_12381.pdf?sequence=1&isAllowed=y.

5. For the pre-2011 literature on Al Jazeera, see, e.g., Mohammed El-Nawawy and
Adel Iskandar, *Al Jazeera: How the Free Arab News Network Scooped the World and
Changed the Middle East* (Cambridge, MA: Westview Press, 2002); Hugh Miles, *Al-
Jazeera: The Inside Story of the Arab News Channel that Is Challenging the West* (New
York: Grove Press, 2005). On Al Jazeera and the Arab spring, see Sam Cherribi, *Days
of Rage: Al Jazeera, the Arab Spring, and Political Islam* (New York: Oxford University
Press, 2017); Ezzeddine Abdelmoula, *Al-Jazeera and Democratization: The Rise of the
Arab Public Sphere* (New York: Routledge, 2015).

6. Compare Yassine Temlali, "The 'Arab Spring': Rebirth or Final Throes of Pan-
Arabism?" *Perspectives* 2, no. 6 (2011): 46–49, https://ps.boell.org/sites/default/files
/downloads/Perspectives_02–06_Yassine_Temlali1.pdf.

7. Edmund S. Morgan, *Inventing the People: The Rise of Popular Sovereignty in
England and America* (New York: W. W. Norton, 1988).

8. Compare the diverse collection of essays in Alain Badiou et al., *What Is a People?*
(New York: Columbia University Press, 2016).

9. See Judith Butler, *Notes Toward a Performative Theory of Assembly* (Cambridge,
MA: Harvard University Press, 2015); Judith Butler, "'We the People': Thoughts on
Freedom of Assembly," in *What Is a People?* ed. Badiou et al. (New York: Columbia
University Press, 2016), 49, 55–59. See also Amira Taha and Christopher Combs,
"Of Drama and Performance: Transformative Discourses of the Revolution," in *Trans-
lating Egypt's Revolution: The Language of Tahrir*, ed. Samia Mehrez (Cairo: American
University in Cairo Press, 2012), 69.

10. See Georges Lefebvre, *The French Revolution: From Its Origins to 1793* (London: Routledge, 2005), and in particular chapter 8 ("The Popular Revolution"),
112–30.

11. Compare Laura Gribbon and Sarah Hawas, "Signs and Signifiers: Visual Translations of Revolt," in *Translating Egypt's Revolution*, 119.

12. The English phrase "will of the people" in association with Parliament can already be found as early as 1689, when it was used twice by Henry Vane, *The Cause of
the People of England Stated* (London: Richard Baily, 1689), 12, 15. Earlier medieval
usage of *voluntas populi* (in contrast) typically related to the justification for why cus-
tom may be considered a source of law: because it reflects the consent of the people
(*consensus populi*) or the will of the people (*voluntas populi*). See Serena Ferente,
"Late Medieval Sovereignty in Marsilius and the Jurists," in *Popular Sovereignty in
Historical Perspective*, ed. Richard Bourke and Quentin Skinner (Cambridge: Cambridge University Press, 2016), 111.

13. John Locke, *The Second Treatise of Government*, in Locke, *Two Treatises of Government* (Cambridge: Cambridge University Press, 1988), 267.

14. *Al-jaysh wa-l-sha'ab yad wahda*, or in Egyptian colloquial Arabic, *al-gish wa-l-sha'b id wahda*. On this slogan, dating at least to January 28, 2011, see Menna Khalil, "The People and the Army Are One Hand: Myths and Their Translations," in *Translating Egypt's Revolution*, 249, 256–60. Khalil notes that the order of the "army" and the "people" was sometimes reversed in the chanted slogan. See also Neil Ketchley, "'The Army and the People Are One Hand!' Fraternization and the 25th January Egyptian Revolution," *Comparative Studies in Society and History* 56, no. 1 (2014): 155–86. See also John Rees, "The People and the Army Are Not One Hand," *Counterfire*, July 2, 2013, http://www.counterfire.org/articles/analysis/16547-egypt-the -people-and-the-army-are-not-one-hand. ("The MB demonstrators were chanting 'the army and the people are one hand': that is they were appealing to the army to intervene and save the government.")

15. Roger Owen, *The Rise and Fall of Arab Presidents for Life* (Cambridge, MA: Harvard University Press, 2014).

16. Imen Gallala-Arndt, "Constitutional Reforms in Tunisia, Egypt, Morocco and Jordan: A Comparative Assessment," *IEMed Mediterranean Yearbook Med.2012* (Barcelona: European Institute of the Mediterranean [IEMed], 2012), http://www.iemed .org/observatori-en/arees-danalisi/arxius-adjunts/anuari/med.2012/gallala_en.pdf.

17. Of course, it is also important to note that the term "democracy" is itself subject to different interpretations in different contexts. Polls from 2011 and 2017 suggest that to most Egyptians, the core elements of "democracy" were socioeconomic rather than political or procedural. See Arab Barometer, June 2011, http://www.arabbarometer .org/wp-content/uploads/Egypt_Public_Opinion_Survey_2011.pdf; Arab Barometer, July 2017, http://www.arabbarometer.org/wp-content/uploads/Egypt _Public_Opinion_Survey_2016.pdf.

18. See, e.g., Perry Cammack, Michele Dunne, Amr Hamzawy, Marc Lynch, Marwan Muasher, Yezid Sayigh, and Maha Yahya, *Arab Fractures: Citizens, States, and Social Contract* (Washington, DC: Carnegie Endowment for International Peace, 2016), https://carnegieendowment.org/2017/02/01/arab-fractures-citizens-states -and-social-contracts-pub-66612.

19. Public opinion polls are of some limited use in sustaining my argument, but as a source of evidence they can be interpreted to support various inconsistent positions. Consider, for example, a 2010 Gallup poll, "Egyptians', Tunisians' Well-Being Plummets Despite GDP Gains," https://news.gallup.com/poll/145883/Egyptians -Tunisians-Wellbeing-Plummets-Despite-GDP-Gains.aspx. The Gallup data show that between 2005 and 2010, the number of Egyptians reporting themselves as "thriving" (in Gallup's formula) declined from 29% to 12%. For Tunisians, the decline between 2008 and 2010 was from 24% to 14%. Yet at the same time, GDP increased

in both countries. These data could be used to argue that there was no social contract operative; but they could also be used to claim that the social contract was losing its grip. Another Gallup poll shows significant decline in satisfaction with government in Egypt between 2009 and 2010. But conditions had not changed appreciably in that year. So is this evidence of a collapsing social contract or of the recognition that no such contract existed? "Egypt: The Arithmetic of Revolution," https://news.gallup .com/poll/157043/egypt-arithmetic-revolution.aspx.

Chapter 2: Tahrir and the Problem of Agency

1. "Hosni Mubarak's Speech to the Egyptian People: 'I Will Not . . . Accept to Hear Foreign Dictations,'" Thursday, February 10, 2011, 4:50 p.m., http://www .washingtonpost.com/wpdyn/content/article/2011/02/10/AR2011021005290.html.

2. "Text of Omar Suleiman's Address," *New York Times*, February 11, 2011, http:// www.nytimes.com/2011/02/12/world/middleeast/12-suleiman-speech-text.html.

3. See Arendt, *The Human Condition*, 175–247.

4. This despite the fact that the internationally recognized Iraq-Syria border is not the one proposed on the Sykes-Picot maps. See Sara Pursley, "'Lines Drawn on an Empty Map': Iraq's Borders and the Legend of the Artificial State (Part 1)," *Jadaliyya*, June 2, 2015, http://www.jadaliyya.com/Details/32140/%60Lines-Drawn-on-an -Empty-Map%60-Iraq%E2%80%99s-Borders-and-the-Legend-of-the-Artificial-State -Part-1.

5. "Obama Says Egypt's Transition 'Must Begin Now,'" February 2, 2011, 8:51 a.m. EST, http://www.cnn.com/2011/POLITICS/02/01/us.egypt.obama/index.html.

6. Gallup, "Egyptians' Views of Government Crashed before Overthrow," https:// news.gallup.com/poll/163796/egyptian-views-government-crashed-overthrow.aspx.

7. Indeed, almost a year later, in April 2014, a Pew poll found that 54% supported the removal of Morsi while 43% opposed it. Pew, "One Year after Morsi's Ouster, Divides Persist on El-Sisi, Muslim Brotherhood," http://www.pewglobal.org/2014/05 /22/one-year-after-morsis-ouster-divides-persist-on-el-sisi-muslim-brotherhood/. Perhaps not by coincidence, by a similar 54–44% margin, Egyptians told the same poll that stability was superior to democracy.

8. For a less metaphorical, historically informed account of the tango, including various models for describing both sides' behavior, see Omar Ashour, "Collusion to Crackdown: Islamist-Military Relations in Egypt," Brookings Doha Center Analysis Paper, March 2015, https://www.brookings.edu/wp-content/uploads/2016/06/en -collusion-to-crackdown.pdf.

9. See Carrie Rosefsky Wickham, *The Muslim Brotherhood: Evolution of an Islamist Movement* (Princeton: Princeton University Press, 2013), 254–56. To understand how

the army shaped the judicial process, consider, for example, that on April 25, before the presidential elections, the assembly speaker Sa'ad Al-Katatni stated that Prime Minister Kamal Al-Ganzouri, appointed by the army, had told him that "the ruling to dissolve the Parliament is in the drawer of the Constitutional Court." The statement reflects the belief by the Brotherhood that the army was pressuring or controlling the court. See Ashour, "Collusion to Crackdown," 27.

10. Wickham, *The Muslim Brotherhood,* 256.

11. Wickham points out that in the first round, two other candidates, the Nasserist Hamdeen Sabahi and the former Brotherhood member Abdel Moneim Aboul Fotouh, jointly won nearly 40% of the vote, more than either Morsi or Shafiq. Her argument is that this shows the revolutionary split facilitated Morsi's success (ibid., 258). But it could also be argued that Aboul Fotouh's voters were moderately supportive of the Brotherhood and voted for Morsi in the second round. See also pp. 264–66 on the second round.

12. On this event, and "the war of attrition between the SCC and the Morsi regime," see Sahar F. Aziz, "(De)liberalizing Judicial Independence in Egypt," in *Egypt and the Contradictions of Liberalism: The Illiberal Intelligentsia and the Future of Egyptian Democracy,* ed. Dalia F. Fahmy and Daanish Faruqi (London: Oneworld, 2017), 85, 106–7.

13. Hesham Sallam argued at the time that the army was divided and that the change could not have succeeded "without the support, if not the leadership of senior military officials." Hesham Sallam, "Morsy, the Coup and the Revolution: Reading between the Red Lines," *Jadaliyya,* August 15, 2012, http://www.jadaliyya .com/Details/26882/Morsy,-the-Coup-and-the-Revolution-Reading-between-the -Red-Lines; see Wickham, *The Muslim Brotherhood,* 269–70. A similar theory, with a generational twist, is described in Eric Trager, *Arab Fall: How the Muslim Brotherhood Won and Lost Egypt in 891 Days* (Washington, DC: Georgetown University Press, 2016), 160–61.

14. Trager, *Arab Fall,* 160, also reports a false rumor that Sisi's wife actually wore the niqab, a rumor mentioned by Zeinab el-Gundy, "Meet General el-Sisi, Egypt's Defence Minister," *Al-Ahram Online,* August 13, 2012, http://english.ahram.org.eg /NewsContent/1/0/50305/Egypt/0/Meet-General-ElSisi,-Egypts-defence -minister.aspx. If this had been true it would have been astonishing, and it is highly unlikely to have been believed by the Brotherhood. It is more likely to have been spread by Sisi's enemies who were suggesting at the time that he was in league with the Brotherhood.

15. On Sisi's *zabiba,* see Marina Ottaway, "Egyptians Uncertain about Future under President Sisi," BBC News, July 3, 2014, https://www.bbc.com/news/world -middle-east-28126198.

16. Mohamed Abdel-Baky, "Rached Al-Ghannouchi: Morsi Victory Announces Death of Mubarak Regime," *Al-Ahram Online*, June 30, 2012, http://english.ahram.org .eg/NewsContent/2/8/46581/World/Region/Rached-AlGhannouchi-Morsi -victory-announces-death-.aspx; David Hurst, "Muslim Brotherhood Urged to Share Power in Egypt," *Guardian*, June 12, 2012, https://www.theguardian.com/world /2012/jun/12/muslim-brotherhood-share-power-egypt.

17. Nadeen Shaker, "In Cairo, Al-Ghannouchi Warns against 'Democracy of the Majority,'" *Al-Ahram Online*, June 4, 2013, http://english.ahram.org.eg/NewsContent /2/8/73167/World/Region/In-Cairo,-AlGhannouchi-warns-against-democracy -of-.aspx, cited and discussed in Monica Marks, "Tunisia," in *Rethinking Political Islam*, ed. Shadi Hamid and William McCants (Oxford: Oxford University Press, 2017), 37.

18. David D. Kirkpatrick, "Egypt Court Strikes a Decree Reimposing Martial Law," *New York Times*, June 26, 2012, http://www.nytimes.com/2012/06/27/world /middleeast/egypt-court-suspends-decree-imposing-martial-law.html. For the claim that the SCAF was directing the action of the constitutional court, see David D. Kirkpatrick, "Judge Helped Egypt's Military to Cement Power," *New York Times*, July 3, 2012, https://www.nytimes.com/2012/07/04/world/middleeast/judge-helped -egypts-military-to-cement-power.html?smid=nytcore-ios-share. Tahani el-Gebali, deputy president of the constitutional court, later disputed the comments she gave to the paper, which stood by its story.

19. The decree is sometimes depicted as the inflection point where Morsi's support declined. Gallup found that Morsi's support was at 57% in November 2012 and declined precipitously thereafter. Gallup, "Egyptians' Views of Government Crashed before Overthrow," https://news.gallup.com/poll/163796/egyptian-views -government-crashed-overthrow.aspx.

20. Kirkpatrick, "Egypt Court Strikes a Decree Reimposing Martial Law"; Kirkpatrick, "Judge Helped Egypt's Military to Cement Power."

21. Fahmy and Faruqi, eds., *Egypt and the Contradictions of Liberalism*, 1–30.

22. Ibid., 2.

23. Ibid., 5.

24. Ibid., 6.

25. See also John L. Esposito, Tamara Sonn, and John O. Voll, *Islam and Democracy after the Arab Spring* (Oxford: Oxford University Press, 2016), 231–32, referring to Egypt's secular intelligentsia as "faux liberals" and arguing that liberals "not only embraced Morsi's ousting but also welcomed violent crackdowns on the group and hailed the ensuing military." The authors single out Mohamed ElBaradei, the former head of the International Atomic Energy Agency and one-time liberal presidential candidate, and the feminist intellectual Nawal El-Saadawi.

Chapter 3: Syria and the Question of Fault

1. See Yaron Friedman, *The Nuṣayrī-ʿAlawīs: An Introduction to the Religion, History and Identity of the Leading Minority in Syria* (Leiden: Brill, 2010).

2. Nir Rosen, "A Tale of Two Syrian Villages," Al-Jazeera, October 26, 2011, https://www.aljazeera.com/indepth/features/2011/10/20111023102856446977.html. Notably, the source quoted in the article denies that Sunnis have chanted the slogan: "'Alawites say we will throw them into the sea but nobody in the opposition ever said 'Alawites to the coffin and Christians to Beirut,' he said. Khaled, however, admitted that the opposition was almost entirely Sunni. 'One out of 10,000 Alawites are in the opposition,' he said. 'Maybe 200 in total, and they are all known by name.'" See also Simon Adams, "The World's Next Genocide," *New York Times*, November 15, 2012, http://www.nytimes.com/2012/11/16/opinion/the-worlds-next-genocide.html. Note that as of late 2012, the fear of genocide expressed by the op-ed writer, head of an organization called the Global Centre for the Responsibility to Protect, was for the 'Alawis, not Sunni civilians or minorities later subjected to genocidal attacks by the Islamic State. I owe this point to Gal Koplewitz.

3. David W. Lesch, "Anatomy of an Uprising: Bashar al-Assad's Fateful Choices that Launched a Civil War," in *The Arab Spring: The Hope and Reality of the Uprisings*, 2nd ed., ed. Mark L. Haas and David W. Lesch (Boulder, CO: Westview Press, 2017), 91, 92, 98–101.

4. Ibid., 101.

5. See, e.g., Worth, *A Rage for Order*, 80–81.

6. A prime example is the 'Alawi anti-regime activist and writer Samar Yazbek, author of *A Woman in the Crossfire: Diaries of the Syrian Revolution*, trans. Max Weiss (London: Haus Publishing, 2012). See Worth, *A Rage for Order*, 90–92.

7. See, e.g., Michael Hastings, "Inside Obama's War Room: How He Decided to Intervene in Libya—and What It Says about His Evolution as Commander in Chief," *Rolling Stone*, October 13, 2011, https://www.rollingstone.com/politics/politics-news/inside-obamas-war-room-238074/.

8. See Edward N. Luttwak, "In Syria, America Loses if Either Side Wins," *New York Times*, August 24, 2013, https://www.nytimes.com/2013/08/25/opinion/sunday/in-syria-america-loses-if-either-side-wins.html ("At this point, a prolonged stalemate is the only outcome that would not be damaging to American interests").

9. The song "Yallah irhal ya bashar!" competed with a pro-Assad song lyric, *nahna rijalak ya bashar!* ("We are your men, O Bashar!"). See, e.g., Robert Mackey, "Video of Syrian Protest Anthem," July 21, 2011, https://thelede.blogs.nytimes.com/2011/07

/21/video-of-a-syrian-protest-anthem/. For a longer version of the song, see https://
www.youtube.com/watch?v=xCS8SsFOBAI. For the pro-Assad song, see https://
www.youtube.com/watch?v=bDkR2KG_7x0.

10. I have argued that the root cause of the Syrian civil war was the structure of the
'Alawi regime. In order to test that hypothesis, it is worth considering the two other
civil wars that followed the Arab spring: those in Libya and in Yemen. In neither case
was the autocratic regime that preceded the Arab spring in the sole possession of a
dominant minority, as it was in Syria. In both cases, however, the collapse of the old
regime led to the emergence—or rather, reemergence—of different factions that had
been more or less successfully suppressed under the banner of nationalism, much as
in Syria. In Libya, the factions that emerged were at first tribal, then regional and, to
an extent, ethnic-linguistic. Religious-political ideology played a subordinate but
meaningful role. The two main actors in the war's second iteration received support
from different external actors, but the civil war never took on a truly transnational
character. The current, third iteration of the struggle—not fully violent as of this
writing—seems to have no ideological content at all and features the efforts of General Khalifa Haftar of the Libyan National Army to establish his own one-man rule
over the country. In Yemen, the factions were regional and Islamic
denominational—Sunni versus Zaydi—as well as tribal. The Yemeni civil war has
gradually been transformed into a proxy war between Saudi Arabia and Iran, the dominant Sunni and Shi'i regional powers. In this way it has come to resemble the Syrian
civil war, with the major difference that no winner has yet emerged.

11. UNHCR estimates of January 2019. See https://www.unhcr.org/syria
-emergency.html.

Chapter 4: The Islamic State as Utopia

1. Feldman, *What We Owe Iraq*.

2. Ibid., 71–82, where I describe the emergence of ethnic and denominational
divisions.

3. See Cole Bunzel, "From Paper State to Caliphate: The Ideology of the Islamic
State," Brookings Project on U.S. Relations with the Islamic World, Analysis Paper
No. 19, March 2015, https://www.brookings.edu/wp-content/uploads/2016/06/The
-ideology-of-the-Islamic-State.pdf.

4. The best-detailed account available at present is Charles R. Lister, *The Syrian
Jihad: Al-Qaeda, the Islamic State and the Evolution of an Insurgency* (Oxford: Oxford
University Press, 2015). I have relied on Lister's chronology here.

5. Feldman, *After Jihad*, 7.

6. In 2016, Ghannouchi self-consciously redefined himself and his party as "Muslim Democrats" rather than "Islamists" committed to "political Islam." See Rached Ghannouchi, "From Political Islam to Muslim Democracy," *Foreign Affairs*, September/October 2016, https://www.foreignaffairs.com/articles/tunisia/political -islam-muslim-democracy.

7. Feldman, *Fall and Rise of the Islamic State*.

8. As Cole Bunzel has argued, the Islamic State ideology was also in important ways Wahhabi, reflecting not the Wahhabism of contemporary Saudi Arabia but that of Muhammad Ibn ʿAbd al-Wahhab himself. See Cole Bunzel, "The Kingdom and the Caliphate: Duel of the Islamic States," Carnegie Endowment for International Peace, February 18, 2016, https://carnegieendowment.org/2016/02/18 /kingdom-and-caliphate-duel-of-islamic-states-pub-62810.

9. I do not intend to embrace this analysis. See my description in Feldman, *Fall and Rise of the Islamic State*, 92–102, and see David Dean Commins, *Islam in Saudi Arabia* (London: I. S. Tauris, 2015).

10. For the argument that the Bolshevik Revolution was not only revolutionary but also effectively religious-reformist despite its secularism, see Yuri Slezkine, *The House of Government: A Saga of Revolutionary Russia* (Princeton: Princeton University Press, 2017). Slezkine also offers a characteristically sweeping, brilliant, and overstated narrative of such religious-revolutionary movements from the time of Jesus to the twentieth century.

11. *Inna allaha yabʿathu le-hadhihi al-ʾummati ʿala raʾsi kulli miʾati sanatin man yujaddidu laha dinatiha. Sunan Abi Daʾud*, No. 4278; in some editions, No. 4291. Chapter location varies from 37–39 by edition.

12. For a close reading of the declaration, see David J. Wasserstein, *Black Banners of ISIS: The Roots of the New Caliphate* (New Haven: Yale University Press, 2017), 3–55.

13. Norman Cohn, *The Pursuit of the Millennium: Revolutionary Millenarians and Mystical Anarchists of the Middle Ages* (Oxford: Oxford University Press, 1970).

14. Stephen F. Cohen, *Bukharin and the Bolshevik Revolution: A Political Biography, 1888–1938* (Oxford: Oxford University Press, 1980), 167.

15. Valeria Cetorelli, Isaac Sasson, Nazar Shabila, and Gilbert Burnham, "Mortality and Kidnapping Estimates for the Yazidi Population in the Area of Mount Sinjar, Iraq, in August 2014: A Retrospective Household Survey," *PLOS Medicine*, May 9, 2017, https://doi.org/10.1371/journal.pmed.1002297.

16. Wasserstein, *Black Banners of ISIS*, 175; see also Rukmini Callamachi, "Freed from ISIS, Yazidi Women Return in 'Severe Shock,'" *New York Times*, July 2017, https://www.nytimes.com/2017/07/27/world/middleeast/isis-yazidi-women -rape-iraq-mosul-slavery.html.

17. Rukmini Callamachi, "ISIS Enshrines a Theology of Rape," *New York Times*, August 2015, https://www.nytimes.com/2015/08/14/world/middleeast/isis -enshrines-a-theology-of-rape.html?_r=0.

18. The controversial example of Mahmud of Ghazni in his invasions of the Indian subcontinent is worth exploring.

19. It has been argued that the best way to understand IS destruction of ancient monuments is to treat it as part of IS's more general rejection of nationalism. The basic idea is that the Iraqi nation-state, for example, embraced and preserved antiquities as part of its project of creating a national identity. Since IS rejects the nation-state as a form of idolatry, ancient sites—including old Islamic sites—can thus be associated with idolatry. See Christopher W. Jones, "Understanding ISIS's Destruction of Antiquities as a Rejection of Nationalism," *Journal of Eastern Mediterranean Archaeology & Heritage Studies* 6, no. 1–2 (2018): 31–58. The argument is intriguing if perhaps mildly overstated in requiring IS to have a sophisticated, almost Western-academic understanding of nation-state construction. In any case, it is entirely consistent with my view that IS sought to transcend the nation-state even as it adopted some aspects of state-like bureaucratic behavior.

20. For a differing view, see Graeme Wood, *The Way of the Strangers: Encounters with the Islamic State* (New York: Random House, 2016), and especially Graeme Wood, "What ISIS Really Wants," *Atlantic*, March 2015, https://www.theatlantic .com/magazine/archive/2015/03/what-isis-really-wants/384980/.

21. See Sahih Muslim No. 2897 ("Abu Hurayra reported the Messenger of Allah (peace be upon him) as saying: The hour will not come until the Rum are landed at al-A'maq or at Dabiq. An army of the best of the people of the earth of the day will go out from Medina to them . . .") (translation mine). On Dabiq in Islamic apocalyptic literature, see also Wasserstein, *Black Banners of ISIS*, 177–92. It is worth noting that IS gave up Dabiq ultimately without a major battle.

22. Patricia Zengerle and Jonathan Landay, "CIA Director Says Islamic State Still Serious Threat," Reuters, June 16, 2016, https://www.reuters.com/article/us -mideast-crisis-fighters/cia-director-says-islamic-state-still-serious-threat -idUSKCN0Z21ST.

23. Compare Olivier Roy, *Globalized Islam: The Search for a New Ummah* (New York: Columbia University Press, 2004), 290–321, to Gilles Kepel, *The War for Muslim Minds: Islam and the West* (Cambridge, MA: Harvard University Press, 2004), 108–51. On the rivalry between the two scholars over the "radicalization of Islam" versus the "Islamization of radicalism," see Adam Nossiter, "'That Ignoramus': 2 French Scholars of Radical Islam Turn Bitter Rivals," *New York Times*, July 12, 2016, https://www.nytimes.com/2016/07/13/world/europe/france-radical -islam.html.

24. Cf. Scott Atran, "ISIS Is a Revolution," *Aeon*, December 15, 2015, https://aeon
.co/essays/why-isis-has-the-potential-to-be-a-world-altering-revolution.

25. Scott Mainwaring and Aníbal Pérez-Liñán, *Democracies and Dictatorships in
Latin America: Emergence, Survival, Fall* (Cambridge: Cambridge University Press,
2013), 221–22.

26. For an analysis of writing by female IS recruits and members, see Wasserstein,
Black Banners of ISIS, 129–45: "the women themselves tell us . . . that they go to IS
territory in order to live lives of freedom, as God wishes them to, serving Allah and
preparing for . . . the world to come."

27. One anonymous reviewer of the manuscript for this book denounced this argument as "specious" and asked whether the Nazis were "also attempting to act as agents
in politics every bit as much as those who took part in the American Revolution." The
answer, of course, is certainly yes. It is a cardinal error of political theoretical analysis
only to ascribe political action to those whose methods or actions one endorses.

Chapter 5: Tunisia and Political Responsibility

1. For the best full history in English, see Kenneth Perkins, *A History of Modern
Tunisia*, 2nd ed. (Cambridge: Cambridge University Press, 2014).

2. See, e.g., "US Embassy Cables: Tunisia—a US Foreign Policy Conundrum,"
Guardian, December 7, 2010, https://www.theguardian.com/world/us-embassy
-cables-documents/217138.

3. For comparison, on consensus—with a critical edge—see, e.g., Nadia Marzouki
and Hamza Meddeb, "The Struggle for Meanings and Power in Tunisia after the
Revolution," *Middle East Law and Governance* 8 (2016): 119, 126 ("As a matter of fact,
the invocation of consensus by the Tunisian ruling elite does not reflect a political
and social context of peace and positive adhesion to a popular ideology. Rather it
reveals a precarious equilibrium among fragile political forces that are increasingly
alienated from social forces").

4. Marks, "Tunisia," 39, 319 n. 33. Marks also skillfully discusses the rise of Salafi-
jihadism in Tunisia and government responses (38–46). Hamid, *Islamic Exceptionalism*, 206–14, offers an account of why Tunisians might join IS that is focused on the
newness and superficiality of Tunisian democratization. An alternative is to see the
Tunisian democratic opening as creating space for a new antidemocratic Salafi politics. For a version of this view, see Fabio Merone and Francesco Cavatorta, "The Rise
of Salafism and the Future of Democratization," in *The Making of the Tunisian Revolution: Contexts, Architects, Prospects*, ed. Nouri Gana (Edinburgh: Edinburgh University Press, 2013), 252, 266.

5. I eagerly anticipate such a work by Malika Zeghal, forthcoming from Princeton University Press.

6. On Tunisia's secularism and its relevance to Ennahda, see Shadi Hamid, *Temptations of Power: Islamists & Illiberal Democracy in a New Middle East* (Oxford: Oxford University Press, 2014), 191–94.

7. Nadia Marzouki, "From Resistance to Governance: The Category of Civility in the Political Theory of Tunisian Islamists," in *The Making of the Tunisian Revolution: Contexts, Architects, Prospects,* ed. Nouri Gana (Edinburgh: Edinburgh University Press, 2013), 217.

8. The best account of the event in February 2012 is Agence France Presse, "Union Protestors Call for Tunisia Government to Resign," *Daily Star*, February 25, 2012, http://www.dailystar.com.lb/News/Middle-East/2012/Feb-25/164627-union -protesters-call-for-tunisia-government-to-resign.ashx.

9. This took place on March 16, 2012. See Lin Noueihed, "Tunisian Protesters Demand Islamic State," March 17, 2012, https://www.alarabiya.net/articles/2012/03/17 /201161.html.

10. Marzouki, "From Resistance to Governance," 218. Shadi Hamid, however, relying on a personal interview with conservative Ennahda member Shaykh Habib El-louze, writes that "80 percent vot[ed] 'no' in an internal Shura Council vote" on whether shari'a should be "enshrined in the constitution." Hamid, *Temptations of Power*, 201.

11. See Nadia Marzouki, "Tunisia's Rotten Compromise," *Middle East Research and Information Project,* July 10, 2015, https://www.merip.org/mero/mero071015. As the title of the essay suggests, Marzouki is actually offering a critique of the concept of consensus. She writes: "These terms are assigned positive or negative valence, depending on who is using them and when, in order to bless agreements that advance a party's interests and/or the common good or, by contrast, to condemn deals that imperil a party's interests and/or democratic norms. These rhetorical battles demonstrate the complexity of the debates in Tunisia since 2011, and belie both the deterministic narrative of an arbitration-prone mentality and the Orientalist trope according to which Arab political culture is essentially incompatible with compromise."

12. Cf. Malika Zeghal.

13. In fact, the UGTT at first took a cautious attitude toward what would become the protests, then turned decisively in their favor. For an important account of the UGTT's longer history and role, see Sami Zemni, "From Socio-Economic Protest to National Revolt: The Labor Origins of the Tunisian Revolutions," in *The Making of the Tunisian Revolution: Contexts, Architects, Prospects,* ed. Nouri Gana (Edinburgh: Edinburgh University Press, 2013), 128.

14. Ann M. Lesch, "The Authoritarian State's Power over Civil Society," in *Egypt and the Contradictions of Liberalism: The Illiberal Intelligentsia and the Future of Egyptian Democracy*, ed. Fahmy and Faruqi (London: Oneworld, 2017), 121.

15. Feldman, *What We Owe Iraq*, 52–55.

16. See Zemni, "From Socio-Economic Protest to National Revolt," 136 (describing the "puppet leadership" of UGTT put in place by Bourguiba in 1978); 137–38 (arguing that UGTT backed nearly all Ben Ali decisions under a "policy of neutrality"); Béatrice Hibou, *The Force of Obedience: The Political Economy of Repression in Tunisia* (Cambridge: Polity Press, 2011), 123–24 (writing in 2006) ("Unlike what happened in the 1960s and 1970s, and even the start of the 1980s, the trade union is no longer a vital force these days").

17. See Zemni, "From Socio-Economic Protest to National Revolt," 138. For a variant, pre–Arab spring version of the "social peace" hypothesis, which emphasized the success of Ben Ali in gaining control over the union, see Hibou, *Force of Obedience*, 124, 317n37, citing Sadri Khiari, *Tunisie: Le délitement de la cité: Coercition, consentement, résistance* (Paris: Éditions Karthala, 2003), 33–34.

18. Dafna Hochman Rand, *Roots of the Arab Spring: Contested Authority and Political Change in the Middle East* (Philadelphia: University of Pennsylvania Press, 2013).

19. Cf. Zemni, "From Socio-Economic Protest to National Revolt," 132–40; Hibou, *Force of Obedience*, 95–105.

20. Worth, *A Rage for Order*, 202–21, relies on his excellent reporting to suggest that the personal relationship that Ghannouchi forged between himself and Essebsi played the key role in facilitating the compromise. In Worth's telling, the quartet, which got the Nobel Prize, mostly provided cover for the Ghannouchi-Essebsi deal. "But the national dialogue's heart and soul was the ongoing conversation between Essebsi and Ghannouchi. They were present at almost all meetings, which sometimes went on until dawn" (210). This seems plausible as an account of events on the ground; yet the quartet nonetheless had a structurally crucial part in cementing socioeconomic continuity.

21. "Tunisia President Says Alliance with Moderate Islamists over," AP, September 25, 2018, https://www.apnews.com/9cd28f232b5840f1bfb95c133adf66a3.

22. Zemni, "From Socio-Economic Protest to National Revolt," 140–42, argues that Ennahda would have sought neo-liberal reform in the pathway begun by Ben Ali but that UGTT has held this process back. This is a possible interpretation, although it is worth emphasizing that Ennahda's leadership, especially Ghannouchi, had little in the way of developed economic theory.

23. Compare Hibou, *Force of Obedience*, xxii (arguing for "necessary transformation" of the UGTT in post-revolutionary Tunisia, which on my view has not happened and likely will not).

24. Hibou, *Force of Obedience*, passim, but especially 14–16, 242–66.

25. "Tunisia Rocked by Protests over Price Rises," *Guardian*, January 10, 2018, https://www.theguardian.com/world/2018/jan/10/tunisia-rocked-second-night-protests-over-price-rises-austerity-measures.

26. Max Gallien, "As Tunisia's Political Consensus Cracks, IMF Austerity May Hit the Rocks," *Middle East Eye*, January 19, 2019, https://www.middleeasteye.net/opinion/tunisias-political-consensus-cracks-imf-austerity-may-hit-rocks.

27. On the latter, see Perkins, *A History of Modern Tunisia*, 148–49.

Afterword: Catharsis?

1. Averroes [Ibn Rushd], *Middle Commentary on Aristotle's Poetics*, trans. Charles Butterworth (Princeton: Princeton University Press, 1986), 93. Cf. Thomas O. Beebee, "What the World Thinks about Literature," in *Futures of Comparative Literature: ACLA State of the Discipline Report*, ed. Ursula K. Hesie (New York: Routledge, 2017), 61, 63.

INDEX

Aflaq, Michel, 80
agency. *See* historical agency; political
  agency
'Alawis: Arab nationalism and, 80–82,
  83–84, 95; Ba'thism and, 81–82, 95,
  96; distinct identity of, 79–80;
  empires with influence on, 95–96;
  Iran-Syria alliance and, 83–84; as
  minority dominating Syrian regime,
  xviii, 78, 81–82, 85, 86, 95, 173n10;
  only 15% of Syrian population, 81;
  possible alternative U.S. policies
  and, 93–94
Algeria: protesters achieving removal
  of dictator, 159–61
Al Jazeera, 4, 137
Al Qaeda: foreign volunteers joining,
  117–19, 120; Islamic State compared
  to, 101, 117–18, 120, 124, 125; Jabhat
  al-Nusra and, 107
Al Qaeda in Mesopotamia, 103, 106
Antonius, George, 80
apocalyptic thought. *See* millenialism
Arabic media, 4–5
Arab independence movements,
  anticolonial, xii, 39
Arab nationalism: of 'Alawis, 80–82,
  83–84, 95; assassinations in Tunisia
  and, 142; call for overthrow of

regimes and, 28–29; changed
  since Arab spring, xi, xiii–xv, xviii;
  ideological division among
  Egyptians and, 75–76; non-Sunni
  advocates of, 80–82; the "people" in
  protest slogans and, 1–2, 4. *See also*
  Ba'thism
Arab spring: afterimages in Algeria
  and Sudan, 159–61; alternative
  interpretation of, x–xvii; collapse
  of Arab nation-states as stable
  entities following, 98; collective
  meaning-making in, xxi, xxiii–xxiv,
  8; consensus view of failure, x;
  defined by Arab choice and Arab
  power, xii; distinctively and uniquely
  Arab, 3–4; mostly seeking peaceful
  transition, 14–15, 14n; pessimism
  about Arab politics and, 126–27;
  sparked by Tunisian protests, 155
Arab winter: defined by Arab choice
  and Arab power, xii; lessons of
  tragedy and, 162; not inevitable,
  156–58. *See also* tragedy
Arendt, Hannah, xx–xxii, 39
Aristotle: Arabic commentary on,
  161–62; on free political action, 38;
  on tragedy, x, xxiii, 161–62, 166n18
Arsuzi, Zaki al-, 80